LETTER ᴊᴍ A POSTMAN

A Year of Walking the Walks

TOM DYMOND

Hardstone House

Published by Hardstone House

The events and conversations in this book have been set down to the best of the author's ability.

First paperback edition December 2023

Book design by Andy Bridge
Illustrations by Tallulah Pomeroy
Photography by Stuart Thomas

ISBN 978-1-9169001-1-0

www.tsdymond.com

For my vast array of grandparents.

Donald & Jacqueline, Graham & Rita, Bryan & Clare, and Peter & Jill.

For whom without letters there would not have been love.

CONTENTS

Prologue   1

PART I
WINTER
Letter One   7
Letter Two   12
Letter Three   17
Letter Four   22
Letter Five   26
Letter Six   30
A Short Missive on the Role of a Letterbox   34
Letter Seven   35
Letter Eight   38
Letter Nine   42
Letter Ten   46
A Brace of Short Missives on Failing to Please
Everyone   49

PART II
SPRING
Letter Eleven   53
Letter Twelve   56
Letter Fourteen   60
Letter Fifteen   64
A Short Missive on Dogs in Gardens   68
Letter Sixteen   69
Letter Seventeen   73
Letter Eighteen   76
Letter Nineteen   80
Letter Twenty   84
A Short Missive on the Mystery of the Wolf
Whistle   88

PART III
SUMMER

Letter Twenty-One	93
Letter Twenty-Two	96
Letter Twenty-Three	100
Letter Twenty-Four	104
Letter Twenty-Five	108
A Short Missive on Being Needed	112
Letter Twenty-Six	113
Letter Twenty-Seven	117
Letter Twenty-Eight	122
Letter Twenty-Nine	126
A Short Missive on Dangerous Packages	130
Letter Thirty	131

PART IV
AUTUMN

Letter Thirty-One	139
Letter Thirty-Two	143
Letter Thirty-Three	146
Letter Thirty-Four	149
Letter Thirty-Five	153
Letter Thirty-Six	156
Letter Thirty-Seven	161
Letter Thirty-Eight	164
A Short Missive on the Fate of a Postbox	169
Letter Thirty-Nine	170
A Short Missive on the Whereabouts of Father Christmas	174
Letter Forty	175

PART V
WINTER, ONCE MORE

Letter Forty-One	183
Letter Forty-Two	186
Letter Forty-Three	189
A Short Missive on Reasons to be a Snail	193
Letter Forty-Four	194

Postscript	198
Wrongs of Passage	205
Hooked on the Horizon	207
Reviews	208
Acknowledgements	209
About the Author	211

Perhaps there is no greater test of a man's regularity and easiness of conscience than his readiness to face the postman. Blessed is he who is made happy by the sound of a rat-tat! The good are eager for it; but the naughty tremble at the sound thereof.

William Makepeace Thackeray

PROLOGUE
A LETTER TO THE READER

Dear Reader,

Perhaps you already know, but there is bending, and there is *bending*.

It's among the first lessons one learns as a postie, as one takes to the streets to offload as many letters and parcels as is humanly possible – and on some days a few more than that. Ideally, they will all be offloaded to the correct addresses but – as you have probably noticed – this is not always how it goes.

Occasionally, we do get the right letter to the right house and – knowing what I know now – I believe these small victories could be celebrated with much more gusto than is customary. There is a lot more to being a postie than simply popping the post through the letterbox, for almost every letter or parcel comes with its own specific set of instructions. There is a process for the signed deliveries, of course, and then certain rules for those that can be tracked step by step on your phone, your computer or even your watch these days. But then there is also the more specific and spontaneous instruction often scrawled across a parcel, like *Leave it in this place but by god don't you dare put it there*, or perhaps *Leave with the neighbour with sunflowers in the garden not the one sleeping on a mattress of beer cans on the other side.*

Many items come with the passive-aggressive admonition: *Please do not bend.* It might seem that there is no room for ambiguity within these four words, but posties are a creative bunch when it comes to being told what to do. As far as posties are concerned, what *Please do not bend* on an envelope really means is: *Please do not fold.*

A gentle bending of a letter to fit it through a door is quite alright by us, so long as it is not crinkled, creased or corrupted in some irreversible way. More than that, actually, a gentle bending is a job well done. After all, picture your poor postie bending awkwardly to the level of your letterbox – their heavy satchel dragging them frightfully downward – and imagine their frustration as they remind themselves that the letter currently not fitting through the door is one of many thousands they must deliver that day.

In light of this reminder of the overwhelming daily task with which they are charged, it is only natural for the postie to exercise a little persuasion on the corners of that letter to see that it arrives safely on the inside of your door. This *Please do not bend* letter has travelled many miraculous miles and passed through many hardened hands to find itself outside your house, and it would be such a shame for it not to be in your *own* hands when you return home this evening. Plus, if it doesn't fit today it isn't much more likely to fit tomorrow, when your postie will return with it once more only to find that you've rather inconsiderately gone to work again. And, so I remind myself, as my thumbs push delicately down on the middle of the envelope and my hands ease the edges up to guide said letter harmlessly through... there is bending and there is *bending.*

As I sit at my desk now and pen this letter to you, I see

that even with my postie days behind me this is still a rule worth remembering, for sometimes a good story needs a gentle bending too. Not, I hasten to add, a full-on folding that deems it quite different in shape from that which it was before. There is not a crinkled, creased or corrupted letter that awaits you within this bundle, I promise. No, everything contained in the following letters is a true reflection of my time working as a Royal Mail postman in the city of Bristol. Nothing is bent so out of shape as to be unacceptable to the reader: these letters are delivered faithfully and sincerely. It is just that one or two might have undergone a little persuasion so that they fit through your letterbox, and there is neither a postie nor a writer – dead or alive – who does not know what I mean by that.

Of late it has struck me that the plight of the postie ought to be known. That after some 500 years of them being seen, it is about time that they were heard too. Posties might not be saving lives or educating the next generation, but when a pandemic swept across the world and onto our shores, posties stood shoulder to shoulder on the front line and were seen for what they always have been: key to the functioning of daily society.

Now it's time to hear why they're struggling, and how a bit of banter, a duty of care and a good old sing-song gets them through. Without further ado, allow me to take you by the hand, over the green hills and to the cobbled streets of Bristol: through which I have wandered and wondered.

Your very-gently-post-bending ex-postman,

P.

❦ I ❧
WINTER

Asleep in working Glasgow, asleep in well-set Edinburgh,
Asleep in granite Aberdeen,
They continue their dreams,
But shall wake soon and hope for letters,
And none will hear the postman's knock
Without a quickening of the heart,
For who can bear to feel himself forgotten?

'Night Mail', W. H. Auden

LETTER ONE

24th December

At just before midday this Christmas Eve, passers-by would have heard a strange noise emitting from a parked van on a residential road in south Bristol. An indiscernible hum that somehow seemed both low and high pitched at the same time. It was a noise completely at odds with what one would expect from a parked van, let alone a Royal Mail one.

Perhaps the postie's been beaten up, they might have thought? Unlikely, mind you. This was only Brislington, and one of the less interesting bits at that. It wasn't, say, Knowle West. Even a postie was fair game there: night or day, Christmas or otherwise.

If a passer-by had pressed a nose up to the window – and, truly, I can't tell you how glad I am that they didn't – they would have found a peculiar sight before them. A postie sat perfectly still in the driver's seat, head hanging low and eyes staring intensely at something in their lap. Had it not been for the curious, nondescript noise seeping out of them, they might have thought them asleep, or perhaps worse. It really would have been quite strange for the passer-by. It really was quite strange for me.

You would probably expect Christmas Eve to be the worst day of the year for a postie. That's certainly what I expected as I pulled my aching body out of bed this morning. One last push, I thought, after a certifiably hellish month.

"In at the deep end, then!" the other posties observed to me, when I had started the job a few weeks before.

"I guess so," I replied agreeably, all the while inwardly thinking them dramatic. How hard could it be to post a few letters?

Well, infinitely harder than anybody could have possibly tried to explain to me, it turns out, which is perhaps why nobody ever bothers to try to explain it at all. Forget the deep end, it's like being dropped in the middle of the ocean, where the ocean consists of a never-ending wave of parcels and letters. How it didn't make the news every year – *'Posties break their back daily in December, only for ungrateful public to fall out with their families at Christmas lunch'* – was beyond me, and beyond everyone else too, it seemed. Indeed, *it* was so far beyond everyone's comprehension that I can only assume whatever *it* is, *it* soared right over Bristol and landed somewhere out in the Severn Estuary, where *it* would quietly extinguish and the world would keep on turning on their swivel chairs as they decided what to order online next.

Part of the problem is that this back-breaking work is carried out every year and so is not news anyway, and the other part of the problem is that the people who are doing it (i.e. posties) are too exhausted to report it. If they can muster the strength to lift their house key to their front door at the end of a December day, they simply topple inside and, with a doormat for a pillow, there they sleep. In the morning they wake still in their uniform and ready to re-enter the fray of the sorting office, although first they have to heave themselves out from under a blanket of Christmas letters that their own, less fortunate, postie delivered to them at around 9pm the night before.

In short, it's rather hard being a postie at Christmas. It being my first Christmas in the red uniform, I have found it particularly difficult, hence why when I got up this morning my body was as malleable as one of those packaging tubes, my head as organised as a sack of letters and my ability to think about anything in non-postie terms had long fallen out of my satchel.

And so when I walked into the sorting office this morning and found my colleagues in a state of relaxedness that I had not seen so far in my time there, I wondered if I had slept right through to January. Indeed, for the past four weeks I had been saying a tiny prayer as I entered the sorting office, as if going over the top in some distant and foul war. Pushing reluctantly through the swinging doors I inevitably found the warehouse in a familiar frenzy: a line of idling lorries unloading at the delivery entrance, a mayhem of managers gesticulating and bellowing, and an office floor entirely occupied by parcel-packed trolleys.

This Christmas Eve morning, by contrast, was a disarmingly sedate scene. The lorries had already unloaded our allotted work for the day, the managers were at their desks wearing Christmas hats and uncharacteristic smiles, and for the first time in weeks one could see that the warehouse floor was not a carpet of parcels, but an unsightly industrial grey after all.

I wandered in a daze around to my work station. Awaiting me was only half a box of letters to be sorted – rather than the five or so to which I had become accustomed – and just one measly bag of parcels. Still in a state of considerable confusion I set about robotically putting it all in order, baffled that there was so little to deliver.

By 9am I was out on my rounds – the earliest I have seen the light of day for some time, what with it being defiantly dark when I commute on these winter mornings. A low-hanging sun cut through a crisp winter's morning as beautifully as the birdsong pierced the frosted hedges, there was a peace knitted into the quiet streets and in the cold air, and the pavement felt soft and welcoming as I padded softly down in it in my still stunned state.

It was a matter of when, not if, the strain of the past month would come pouring out of me. In the end, it was the mince pie that did it.

I was on one of my last loops of the round and it still wasn't even midday, and I found myself in sprightly spirits that I had forgotten could be a part of one's existence. A middle-aged man answered his door before I could even get down the garden path and with a big grin he thrust the tear-inducing pastry into my suddenly trembling hands. I didn't know what to say – I hope to the heavens I squeaked some form of thank you – and the man probably thought he had done something gravely wrong. I scuttled back up the garden path and swiftly posted the last few letters in my bundle, before climbing into the driver's seat to sit cradling the mince pie.

The breakdown had been brewing. After weeks of navigating an unfamiliar city in an unbelievably parcel-packed van, delivering to an unapologetically all-consuming public, it was only a matter of time. To be given an achievable amount of work to do on Christmas Eve was one thing, but to be bestowed with this sugary, festive, pastry was too much to bear. That's when strange noises started jumping out of me and tears rolled freely down my cold, pale cheeks, like children's sleighs down snowy hills.

Later that day my sister and her fiancé picked me up on their way through Bristol for our Christmas down south. It was the 'driving home for Christmas' moment of the year. We took a wrong turn and ended up queuing to get over a well-used toll bridge that goes through a little town just outside Bath. We scrounged around the car desperately for enough coins to pay our way over the bridge, but it looked like a lost cause. We'd either have to beg or turn around.

It was then that I remembered the mince pie. It hadn't seemed right to gobble down the only gift that has ever brought me to tears, so I still had it. What did seem befitting, however, was that it could be the currency that got us home for Christmas. We leaned out the window to the wrapped-up toll master, held out our insufficient coins and asked him if, between a little bit of Christmas cheer and a slightly tear-soaked mince pie, he might find space in his heart to let three travellers continue their journey homeward.

The toll master seemed equally moved by the pie. He accepted the pastry gently, cradling it in begloved hands, and as he nodded us through I'm sure I spotted his lower lip start to quiver. It left me wondering if in all of history there ever was such a stirring mince pie as the one that provoked a postman to tears and then built a bridge to home. I like to think the toll master found reason to gift it on once again before the day was done. Or maybe he just ate it.

The work of a postie is brutal: mince pies shouldn't provoke tears. They say that talking helps. I've never been much of one for talking but I don't mind a letter, so here we go.

Yours mincerely,

P.

LETTER TWO

9th January

The HR department of Royal Mail would be pleased to hear that the process by which I became a postie was as smooth as the surface of a crisp white envelope. As long as that crisp white envelope has been left abandoned in the bottom of a damp satchel for weeks, only to subsequently fall out and plop directly into a puddle on the road, where it is swiftly run over by a passing Royal Mail lorry. This once crisp white envelope is then hastily snatched up by a panicked postie who then crumples the now sodden and dirtied paper into a nearby letterbox. Any letterbox will do, for the address has long been rubbed off and the contents of the letter long forgotten by all involved.

I interviewed for the latest vacancy a few months ago, and that so happened to be in Bristol, a city to which I had recently moved. I dug out my one and only suit for the interview, but immediately felt overdressed and regretted it. If you were ever looking to become a postie, incidentally, a more casual dress would probably suffice. It's also worth bearing in mind that for the application process it's prudent to set aside a period of time roughly equivalent to how long Royal Mail advises it takes a parcel to reach Australia (fifteen to eighty business days). Indeed, becoming a postie is a long and vague unfolding, to the point where one wonders if they're actively trying to put off all potential employees.

Anyway, I was very pleased to get the job (as one tends to be), but apprehensive on my first day (as one also tends to be). I turned up precisely when I had been asked to and – more to the point – I turned up precisely *where* I had been asked to. That is, the South Bristol office: the same office to which I had inauspiciously turned up in a suit for my interview and where only the day before I had been informed my employment would commence.

The problem with this, however, was that I was not employed in the South Bristol sorting office at all. That I turned up and tried to offer them my labour was a source of considerable puzzlement to everybody concerned. After a fair share of head scratching and shoulder shrugging it was revealed that I was, in fact, to serve my time in the South*east* Bristol office. This was suddenly very clear to everyone apart from to me, who didn't understand how the organisation in charge of sending things to the right addresses had sent me to the wrong one. Thinking about it with the benefit of hindsight, I now realise that everyone else involved was used to it.

I was, at least, relieved to find that nobody had thought to mention it to the managers at the Southeast office either, for when I showed up there a little later they too were perfectly perplexed by my presence. I was also clearly an unwanted nuisance, for the manager's already taut face tightened a little more as I introduced myself, and he quickly disappeared to find somebody to deal with me. In fairness to him, he was extremely busy pushing paper from one side of his desk to the other, and then back again.

A nice postwoman appeared and gave me a tour of the sorting office: a pulsating and confusing warehouse of frantic letter and parcel sorting. At least two radios were blaring out from opposite corners and dozens of posties chatted loudly between them, although without looking up from their sorting and therefore giving the impression that they weren't talking to each other, but rather were talking to the letters themselves. A steady rifling and swiping of envelopes could just about be made out as they were separated into pigeon holes, and the occasional bang emitted as boxes were dropped to the floor, and trolleys of parcels and post were crashed together. There were pigeons flying around the rafters at the top of the warehouse and if it weren't for the fluorescent lights the whole thing might have felt distinctively Victorian.

"Look at they socks!" A group of posties had gathered around to point at the weathered legs of a combative looking postman, whose garish socks were pulled up as high to his knees as the colourful material would allow. This long-socked postie, who I suspect was of a rather scrappy nature, responded loudly with words that I won't repeat here, and rather predictably only encouraged the now growing group to point and snigger at him. The scene brought back memories of the school playground, and every morning I have spent in the sorting office since has been accompanied by a particular nostalgia for those carefree days.

I received this bemusing tour of my new workplace, not at all understanding the organised chaos before me, to the point where I wondered if this was actually a strike of sorts. It had been in the news a lot at the time, after all. I was then plonked in the canteen and left to my own devices for a bit while they figured out what to do with me next, when all of the posties swiftly burst in for their morning break, still shouting and joking. Nobody paid me much attention for nobody knew who I was or why I was there, but I detected an air of suspicion among them towards this stranger in the room.

One postie sat down nearby, introduced himself and asked what I was about. In my nervousness I went on a long and rambling rant about how they had sent me to the wrong office that morning, a rant that was only lengthened by the deadpan look on his face. Finding myself desperate to enliven his emotionless features I embellished and lengthened my story at each step, but by the time I had reached the end I hadn't inspired so much as a blink, let alone a raised eyebrow.

"Same thing happened to me," he said, taking a sip of his coffee.

"They sent you to the wrong office?" I couldn't believe the coincidence.

"And me," said another postie at the table, suddenly showing interest in our conversation. "Happened to Deano too," he added, nodding over to another postie in the corner. I looked disbelievingly from one to the other.

"You can get used to that level of organisation," the postie next to me declared. "If you stick around, that is," he added ominously.

And with that, as if to the toll of a bell only they could hear, they all stood as one, and shuffled out of the canteen and back into the warehouse. I sat there and wondered if anybody else had noticed the irony of Royal Mail sending their staff to the wrong addresses. It didn't give me a whole lot of hope for the letters.

I spent the rest of that morning on my own in the canteen watching introductory videos that spoon fed me ways of staying alive. In particular, I recall the eight minutes of my life I lost to learning about the benefits of using a handbrake when parking the postvan.

As I was watching these videos I overheard snatches of the bedlam in the adjoining warehouse. The Beatles were playing on the radio, and the whole warehouse was singing along:

"All you need is SOCKS, doo do-do-do doo!"

It had been a strange day. Perhaps the strangest thing, though, was seeing all these postmen and women together. It had never occurred to me that these lone creatures might all be in the same place at the same time at some point of their day, but here they all were. They were quite a force to be reckoned with.

Rock 'n' roll,

P.

LETTER THREE

10th January

When I arrived at the sorting office the next day in late October of last year, it was clear that all memory of my being had been wiped from the managers' minds. Upon seeing me they frowned and even above the early raucous of the warehouse I could hear the cogs of their brains grinding while they tried to place me. When they realised I was the new guy there was a brief moment of relief across their faces. But the question of what to do with me came hot on its heels, and so the audible cogs started grinding once more.

Mercifully, Royal Mail do not simply throw a uniform on you and send you out to the streets cluelessly clutching letters. (It would actually be many weeks before anyone thought to order me some uniform, and so for a long time residents of southeast Bristol scratched their heads as to why a short guy in jeans was fumbling letters through their letterboxes). But Royal Mail do rather make a song and a dance about the training required to do the job. I had already gleaned from yesterday's inane videos that this is not so much part of personal development for the posties, but more to minimise the chance of the Royal Mail company being sued for negligence. As such, the next step on the road to postie-hood was to shadow a fully fledged professional for the day.

I followed a manager around the edges of the warehouse beneath the bright fluorescent lights. In the far corner a red-haired postwoman was introduced to me as Patricia, the office trainer. She smiled at me with the well-practised sweetness of a customer-facing expert, before turning to the manager – daggers sparkling from her eyes – and asked what was going on.

"He needs training," the manager replied curtly, "he'll be following you around today." And with that, he turned on his heel. She sent some more eye-daggers at his back and spent a moment composing herself before turning to me. I shuffled on my feet, searching to find as apologetic a stance as I could, before realising no such position existed, and so I simply stood still – awkwardly.

"This is a frame," she began, somewhat defeatedly, gesturing to the desk behind her, "it's where we prepare our rounds."

The warehouse was full of these so-called frames. They were all identical and lined up in a neat back-to-back fashion, like aisles in a supermarket. Frames are basically desks standing about half-a-metre off the ground, with a stack of shelves that sit at the back of them. There are four rows of these shelves atop each desk and – as they are designed to hold letters – across each shelf are dozens of plastic dividers, creating slots at one-centimetre intervals. To the uninitiated, they look terrifyingly complicated.

"Each of the slots is normally one house," Patricia said, "although on the heavier rounds, sometimes it's two houses squished into one slot. Understand?"

I nodded slowly, and therefore lied.

"We put the letters," she brandished a letter from a letter-stuffed box, presumably because I looked like 5'6" of idiot and she wanted to make sure I at least knew what a letter was, "into the appropriate slot. You find the appropriate slot, by looking at the road names and numbers just below each row. Can you see where this is going?" She tilted her head slightly to the side in mock condescension.

To my own surprise, I could. Each address had its own slot, its own centimetre, so the idea was to put the letters in their allotted centimetre on the shelves. But my mind was quickly zooming out from the one centimetre where her finger was prodding, to the many centimetres along the rest of that row, and to the three other rows that were stacked on the desk.

"How many addresses are on this round?" I blurted abruptly, as the enormity of the task began to unpack itself before me.

"This is a more forgiving one," she winked, "Why do you think I chose to be a trainer? They start you guys off easy, which means I get it easier all year round."

"This is an easy one?" I didn't like the sound of this.

"It's daunting, but you'll get used to it. Take Russell here," she gestured to the postie at the neighbouring frame who could just about be seen behind a temporary wall of boxes of post and bags of parcels. "Before long you'll be just like him: on the hardest round in the office and merrily singing all morning as you prep the frame."

The radio was blaring out Bob Marley and The Wailers' 'Jammin'. Russell was bawling out his own version of the lyrics:

"We're preppin'!
I wanna prep it with you!

We're preppin', PREPPIN',
And I hope you like preppin' too!"

I wanted to point out that Russell didn't seem entirely in charge of his faculties and that perhaps he should be given an easier round for a while, but Patricia had already moved on.

"And so on top of these rows is where we sort the parcels," she was saying. "Once all the letters are in the frame, we take the bags of parcels and…"

But my mind was still stuck on how many slots there were – how many centimetres there were – and so it was now off and counting them: four rows to each frame… seven columns to each row… twenty slots to each column… that meant… that meant five hundred and… five hundred and sixty slots!

"And once all that's done, you have to do the redirects," Patricia was now saying to me. She must have thought she was still talking to a person, but at this point I was a calculator with limbs.

So, if there are 560 addresses on just this frame, my mind raced, how many are in this office? It looked like there were 16 frames along this aisle, and I'd been marched past three other aisles to get to this one, so that made 64 frames altogether! How many centimetres was that?! Too many to calculate in that moment, that was for sure.[1]

With all of the post in the slots, the parcels stacked precariously but systematically on top of the rows, and other various tasks completed that I had been too busy doing horrific calculations to hear, it was now time to take the whole lot down again and pack it into satchels. It was time to head to the streets.

I had been perfectly unprepared for how much information there would be to take in. But if one steps back and thinks about the operation that Royal Mail take responsibility for each day (apart from Sundays: "No post on Sundays," as Mr Dursley famously observed), *of course* there would be a lot to take in. Millions of bits of paper with words scrawled across them aren't going to magic themselves into the right house as if they were an email. This bastion of the analogue world requires physical and mental work by hundreds of thousands of people every day.

As we left the warehouse later that morning – considerably later than Patricia was hoping for, I suspect – I realised that the chaos of the sorting office I had witnessed only the day before actually masked an orderliness and discipline that the general public can scarcely comprehend. Posties might be skipping around, giggling and pointing out the garishness of a particular pair of socks, but these people were also deeply embedded in a process that achieved something only a centimetre shy of a miracle on a daily basis. I'm not actually sure they comprehend it either.

Miraculously,

P.

[1] I have since done the maths and this makes 35,840 centimetres, or 35,840 postal addresses, in our office. In reality, however, it is far more because almost every frame has at least some rows that squeeze two addresses into one centimetre. In any case, it is almost impossible to be precise because new homes are constantly being built, and old homes are getting divided into flats. Royal Mail has a hard enough time getting enough elastic bands, let alone tracking an ever-changing city.

LETTER FOUR

11th January

It was oddly daunting to be responsible for somebody else's letters. Who knew the gravity of their contents? News of medical results, matters of inheritance, declarations of love... all potentially within my grasp! I felt the weight of responsibility that stretches back hundreds of years to when young men – in those days, of course, it was only men – first started carrying the King's letters across the country.

This is, by the way, how Royal Mail began: mailing the royal letters. Specifically, it was Henry VIII who set up the 'Master of the Posts' in 1512, presumably because he required a sizeable network to maintain communications with all his wives. It took about another century before it was decided this whole thing would be called 'Royal Mail', and another two centuries before it was begrudgingly accepted that it might benefit the general public too, not just the aristocracy. I wish I could say that Royal Mail's ability to move with the times has improved as this great institution has aged, but this would be something of an untruth.

As a new postie, I should have partnered with Patricia for the whole of the next week and then been kept on the same round – or 'walk' as posties tend to refer to it – for the next three weeks after that. This procedure, I quickly learned, is never followed because there is never enough staff to allow for it. Indeed, after just one day following a trainer, the management invariably decide that this is quite enough experience. The new starter is hastily chucked onto a different walk, with management citing 'staff shortages and unexpectedly busy days' as reasons that this unfortunate decision has to be taken.

I couldn't understand the posties' anger at this to begin with. I was just keen to get stuck in and prove I wasn't as useless as first impressions had suggested. But once you've been around a little while you begin to understand that 'staff shortages and unexpectedly busy days' are stamped into the system. A system deliberately understaffed and designed to eke out every moment of labour from you, whether you've been in the company five minutes or five decades.

"Now, number 56," my latest postie partner said to me as we prepared his frame on my third morning in the warehouse, "they're *always* in. We'll pop that parcel in yer bag, and you'll be rid of it, no problem."

Neil was the longest serving postie in our office: he'd been a postie for 47 years and counting. There I was, staring at his frame of hundreds of addresses simply trying to remember what my own name was, and Neil could pick out a specific house and tell me what they had for breakfast.

"This lady always leaves her porch open so we can just chuck it in," he went on, referring to the parcel for 72, "and these people 'ere has a dog – bit Andy over there few years back – so give the gate a good rattle before you get in the garden."

I made a desperate mental note of which one had the dog,

but forgot it almost immediately. There was too much to take in. The next parcel he pulled out of the bag was quite small and he stared at it for a few moments, muttering to himself. He caught me watching him. "I ain't mad," he explained, "I'm just trying to remember the size of number 35's letterbox. Yeah, I reckon this parcel'll go through it." And so he slotted it into the frame, having returned from his mind palace where he stored away all this banal but essential postie wisdom.

Posties seem to have an infinite amount of detail tucked away about the people that they serve, and they also seem to feel like that is precisely what they are doing: serving the people. Perhaps I shouldn't generalise about tens of thousands of posties across the country like that... perhaps many don't feel like that at all. But it certainly seems like a lot of them do because, by and large, they're passionate about doing right by the people. Maybe that's why they're always smiling?

I managed to wipe the smile off Neil's face that day as we trudged around Whitchurch. While he knew every person in every house on every street, I knew just two streets in Bristol: one of which I lived on, one of which I worked on, and neither of which were in Whitchurch.

"How did you end up there?" He would cry in genuine despair, as I appeared between two houses that were firmly on his half of the round. "I didn't even know you could get through there!" I looked back at the way I had come and realised I had done more than a little trespassing.

More than once that day I arrived back at the van to find him having a little doze in the driver's seat. He must have finished his loop – as these segments are called – some time before me, and while waiting for me to return he had fallen asleep. I was evidently very slow, and as the clock reached towards 5pm I sensed that – as patient and lovely as he was –

Neil had rather had enough of me. Generally speaking, posties expect to be home in time for an afternoon nap, and while Neil did get several of these, none of them were at home.

Anyway, he was a gentle fellow and didn't bear a grudge, although he did point out that the management had asked too much of me on what was only my second day of posting. My legs were close to collapsing and my brain was as fuzzy as after a night in the pub, so I could only nod meekly at him. As he drove us back to the sorting office I wondered silently how on earth he had managed to do this for 47 years.

Exhaustedly,

P.

LETTER FIVE

21st January

I might have a Christmas under my belt since those first few days when I was new to the job, but I have had to tighten the strap around my waist. Walking eight to ten miles a day will do that to you, even with the weight of Christmas on your back, no matter how many pigs in blankets you squeeze down.

"It don't get no more easy now, mind," Neil warned me when we came back to work after Christmas. "Not just coz that there Christmas is over. We got 'oliday catalogues to deliver all month, now," he said, as he flicked through various cruise holiday options for the year ahead.

When I started working for Royal Mail I was as new to Bristol as I was to posting. I am not a native of this city, well-known for its unique twang: a twang that seems especially to be found among the posties. No, I grew up on the other side of the Mendip Hills in sleepy Dorset, where the twang differed slightly from that of my new neighbours. I could mostly understand what, if you will, were being said, but it does take some getting used to.

Yes, the Bristolian accent – glottal and curious as it is – requires a bit of learnin'. Indeed, G's are often found wantin'; H's 'ave an 'abit of disappearin'; and K's can find their way onto the end of anythingk.

It isn't just letters of the alphabet that the people of Bristol like to shuffle around, but whole words too. An extra 'to' can find its way onto sentences where to it isn't at all needed; additional words often crop up at the end of sentences, mind; and verbs tend to find themselves pluralised, such that they takes so many S's sometimes I thinks the country might runs outs.

Take a conversation from just this morning, between Little Larry, Big Barry and myself. Little Larry and Big Barry went everywhere around the sorting office together, they were as inseparable as milk from tea. As their names suggest, Little Larry is really quite small and Big Barry is really very large, so you wouldn't so much say that they were joined at the hip as joined at the hip and the head. Everyone could see that Little Larry and Big Barry were very good friends, but their chosen manner for demonstrating this was to be veritably ruthless towards one another.

"Where to you postin' today, then?" Little Larry asked me.

"Down to Stockwood today," I answered.

"Eez a long way out innhe, ol' Stockwood," Little Larry observed. "Awlright when ye get to there, mind. Pretty priddy."

"I've never been before," I admitted. "Where are you posting today?"

"Walk firty-free," Little Larry replied. "Ain't too bad. Bit confusin, mind."

Appearing at his side, Big Barry chipped in: "Walk thirty-three, Larry? You'll be lost rounds there won't you?"

"Lost?!" Came the incredulous reply from Larry, who was some 20 years older than Big Barry. "Lost?! I was postin' round there when you woz still in nappies!"

This delighted all those within earshot and laughter erupted all around. Little Larry looked rather pleased, while Big Barry was turning a Royal Mail red. As the chuckles died down, without looking up from his letters and with impeccable timing, Neil quipped: "Jus' last week, then?"

The laughter erupted once more.

My favourite idiosyncrasy of the Bristol accent, is the swapping of the word 'me' for 'I', pronounced *oi*. For example, "gives *oi* that box o' letters" wouldn't be said any other way in a Bristol sorting office. Better still, *oi* appears in many a sing-along too, as do all the other nuances of the Bristol dialect. A sing-along is a feature of most mornings in the sorting office, as if sailors singing shanties on a ship to keep spirits high.

The posties' interpretation of the song 'Higher Love' by Steve Winwood, to take one example, sounds quite different to what one is used to hearing on the radio:

"Bring oi yer 'igher love! Oh!
Bring oi yer 'igher love!
Where to's that 'igher love, I keep thinkin' of!"

While the most pleasing, the local dialect is not the only language I have had to get my head around. As with almost any new job, there is the language of the work to learn as well, the commonplace words in which all the workers are fluent and they toss them around like letters, as though everyone knows them. The tall, square trolleys that transport the boxes of letters and bags of parcels on and off the lorries, for example, are not called trolleys at all, but are rather known as 'Yorks'. This is for the endearingly simple reason that they were made in the city of – you guessed it – York. 'Door-to-doors' refer to junk mail (we're not allowed to call it junk mail, obviously), 'bundles' refer to piles of letters tied up with elastic bands, and 'PDAs' are the electronic devices that we have to scan the parcels with.

Far more challengingly than this, though, is learning the language of the roads. There are hundreds of road names, of course, and they have to be memorised as quickly as possible. As a newcomer to the city it has been difficult enough to understand how the regions in our postcode tie together: where does Totterdown become Knowle, Knowle West become Hengrove, and Whitchurch become Stockwood? As for trying to recall whether Savoy Road, say, is on Walk 38 or 39, well, I've not quite learnt all of that yet it's fair to say.

Oh yes, the Bristol twang is the least of my worries.

Farewell me lover,

P.

P.S. Do you watch the news? I try not to. It's always bad, isn't it? They're making a big thing about how some people in China have died from some virus. Every death is a tragedy and my heart goes out to the families, of course, but do we really need to know about every bad thing that happens in the world?

LETTER SIX

30th January

I pushed through the swinging doors this morning and the warehouse was already in full voice, A-ha's 'Take on Me' pop classic becoming something quite unique through the choir of posties:

"Take ooiiiii on (Take on oi!)
Take on ooiiii! (Take on oi!)
I'll be gone
In a day or twooooooo!"

A choir of posties has a ring to it, don't you think? Since I joined it has intrigued me that there appears to be no common word for a group of posties, but then I also recall my surprise at seeing them all in one place for the first time. The general public will surely never see more than two posties together at any one time, so perhaps there is simply no need for such a word. Personally, however, I think they deserve a collective noun of sorts, and a choir of posties has a nice ring to it. The only trouble is that the English language already has a choir of angels, so it is by no means original and perhaps also not suitable. Posties might be hard workers capable of holding immense amounts of knowledge in their heads, but they are no angels.

"Up the workers!" cried Bert, as he walked down one of the aisles pushing a York.

"Yeah!" A few posties' fists rose in agreement.

"Speaking of which," he turned to them, "'ave you seen any?" Bert winked and carried on down the aisle, letters and insults alike bouncing off his back. That's Bert for you.

Bert works in the back room of the warehouse. He emerges occasionally with nothing but mischievous intent, before retreating into the safety of his lair where he is the keeper of all the so-called 'special' deliveries. They're so special, in fact, that they are kept away by lock and key and we have to queue up each morning to collect and sign for them.

"There ain't much you can do to get in real trouble in this job," Neil told me when I first started, "but for god's sake don't lose a special delivery."

The very next day I did almost exactly that when partnered with a postie who I swiftly came to suspect might murder me. A macho chap and very much one of the leaders among the male-dominated workforce, he was a popular figure. And, unsurprisingly, a nightmare to work with. He saw his round as something that belonged to him personally, and he was fiercely particular about the way things were done on it. With each mistake I made in the sorting process I became more nervous, less competent and further filled with dread for the day ahead. At some point I moved one of these special deliveries without realising it and then we couldn't find it for about half an hour. He grew quietly but unquestionably more incensed, and I began to fear he might tear me open as though an envelope. I was halfway through hastily scrawling down my will on a piece of paper when, mercifully, the special delivery was found. He sat on his haunches to take a few deep breaths, while I slunk away to give him a few minutes to calm down. As I say, posties are no angels.

I had an equally scarring experience with another postie in an entirely different setting, in which he was the customer at home and I was his postman bringing him his parcel.

Still relatively new to the job at the time, I was doing most things by the book. All the posties in the office had told me to throw that book away. "If we did it the way they wanted us," Big Barry had remonstrated, "we wouldn't get the job done until tea time tomorrow." I was realising this more with every working day, but when one is new one has to experiment with which corners can be cut and which corners can lose a job.

I was standing outside in the rain with a parcel that needed signing for. I was knocking and knocking and – keen as I was to do everything by that damned book – I was reluctant to leave without a signature for it in case a manager was watching from a nearby hedgerow. The fellow inside was yelling something at me, but it was muffled and I couldn't hear him through the door, nor over the pitter-patter of the rain. I called back that I was dreadfully sorry, but I needed a signature.

The door was wrenched open, revealing a little man, naked apart from the towel wrapped around his waist. I barely had time to be surprised by this first development, for the second one came smartly after it as he snatched the parcel from my bemused hands. I tried to mumble something about needing a signature, but with his other hand he was already snatching my PDA from me and was scrawling a scribble on the touchscreen.

"I'm. Trying. To. Get." He emphasised each word as he

jotted violently. "In. The. Shower!" he snarled and thrust the device back into my chest. I stood, shocked, but he wasn't done yet. "I been a postie for ten year!" He bellowed in my face. "You don't need a signature! Just bloody scribble on it and leave it outside!"

He slammed the door on me. I stood looking at it in the pouring rain, thoroughly confused. That seemed unnecessary, I thought to myself. Then, as one does after being ambushed, I started framing my retorts to him in my head, thinking all the things I wished I'd been quick enough to say.

"I think you will find, *sir*," was one such thought, "that I am *obliged* to get a signature, as you will well know!" Pathetic, I thought. I tried another: "*Well*, you would hardly have been chuffed to find your parcel left in the rain, would you now?"

The monologue inside my head continued in much the same lame vein for the rest of the day. It is not a good idea to dwell on these things though, and I succeeded only in making a wet and miserable day even more miserable. By the time I got home I was emotionally fatigued from this imaginary argument that in reality I had never shown up for, and had to begrudgingly accept that the only silver lining was that his towel had held up during his gesticulations. It is not pleasant to trudge around in the thankless rain, delivering parcels to such thankless people. I'll win in the long run though: I've remembered his address and shall be crumpling his post from now on.

Yes, a choir of posties would be quite wrong, after all.

Wishing turmoil to your enemies,

P.

P.S. Still banging on about that coronavirus on the news. Just media hype if you ask me.

A SHORT MISSIVE ON THE
ROLE OF A LETTERBOX

Dear Letterbox Makers,

I am just writing to check whether the primary purpose of your product is still to allow bits of paper inside a front door? It's just that you seem to be manufacturing letterboxes with defensive qualities that might match that of the gates of Troy. Thin, wispy slices of material are trying to penetrate these things, not entire Greek armies.

Your nine-fingered postie,

P.

LETTER SEVEN

10th February

The idea of the postie being up and about extraordinarily early, whistling at dawn and delivering letters before breakfast, is strangely persistent. It's been years, maybe decades, since letters routinely landed on the welcome mat before the milk hit the cereal bowl and yet we all still seem to believe that this is the way the world works. In reality posties' working hours have been pushed later and later into the day over the years, and yet the myth that they're the first awake and the first home still prevails.

Until I became one, I myself assumed the same. Despite the afternoon having well established itself before my postie came up the garden path, I continued to assume that the post always arrived at first light. Perhaps the postie I saw in the afternoons, I would vaguely surmise, was the second one today, and I was simply asleep for the arrival of the first. (That this early postie brought me no post at all did not seem to deter me from this theory.)

There did, in fact, used to be multiple deliveries

throughout the day, which I think is astonishing. It used to be that one could write a letter in the morning and hear a reply by the end of the day – by post! In London, as the Industrial Revolution was getting into its stride and businesses were popping up all over town, there was an enormous demand for a postal service throughout the day. Royal Mail stepped in nobly (not to mention profitably) to fill this gap.

Well, not only is there now only one delivery each day, but it's not even guaranteed to arrive before lunch (unless one pays especially for it, that is). When posties are really busy you might even find that you make it home from your nine-to-five job before the letter finds its way onto your doormat. That really is a long way behind the milk hitting the cereal bowl, and as good an indication as any that "it ain't what it used to be", as almost every postie will tell you, including those who have been in the company a whole five minutes longer than me.

As such, it is only on my cycle to work in the morning that I have the streets to myself and even then that is not always the case. Last Saturday morning (we work Saturdays, of course) as I cycled through the damp and shining city centre, a group of young'uns were only just swaying their way home after a night on the sauce. They'd be waking up about the time I finished work later, I'd have guessed. And as society spins 24/7 these days, there were lorry drivers unloading their hauls at the shops, shopworkers sleepily stacking the shelves, and council workers tidying the streets so that people could flock out and litter them once again. The world is too busy now – both in population and in intent – for the streets to ever again be the reserve of just the postie.

Nevertheless, it is still quiet enough at that hour and I enjoy the brisk morning air on my face as I pedal through the silence. Dawn is often a calm time of day with little wind to speak of, and so the air is generally fresh and still. It is a bit of a shame to arrive at the sorting office and to know I will miss the sunrise, as I set to work under the bright white lights of the warehouse, but so it goes.

All the posties tell me that they used to be in the sorting office by 4am, out on their rounds by 6am and back home by lunch. If they weren't home, they were in the pub. Those were the days, they tell me. That does sound good, but I am always wary of the rose-tinted glasses people tend to wear when recounting the past. No doubt back then they were pining for the good old days before that too. It is a strangely universal tendency of humans to think about how the past was always better and the future is always bleak. Perhaps it is because we at least know what happened in the past, whereas the future is always uncertain and that's a scary thing.

As a postie we never know what the day holds until we walk through those swinging doors and behold the volume of mail before us. Some days it is a manageable amount and some days it is not. So I enjoy the city's tranquillity as I cycle to work, before the mayhem ensues.

One last thing. Curiously, many people seem to think that posties still use bicycles on their rounds. In fact, "Do you deliver in a van or on a bike?" is almost always the first thing I am asked when I meet someone and tell them I am a postie. They're referring to the inexplicably famous Pashley Mail-star, but posties haven't used these for years. It's bizarre.

Toodles,

P.

LETTER EIGHT

19th February

In those early morning hours when posties all have their heads down looking at addresses, great interest is taken in the radio. As far as I can glean, a postie's favourite thing is when a song on the radio can be integrated into the goings-on in the office, in one way or another. This might be as simple as getting a bit of a sing-along going to a catchy chorus (*"Soooooooo Sally can wait!"*) or perhaps altering and Bristolising the lyrics in a song for amusement (*"Give-oi, give-oi shelter!"*). Or, as was the case this morning, a song might form the foundations for a serious philosophical discussion.

"How would you feel if the streets had no name?" Big Barry asked Little Larry, as U2's 'Where The Streets Have No Name' blared out on the radio. This earned him a hard stare, for Little Larry took addresses extremely seriously and was one of only a few posties who boasted the remarkable ability to tell you the name of a street just from its postcode. If, for example, a letter came in with a house number and a post-code, but no street name, it would look something like this:

14, Bristol BS14 8LN. Little Larry could tell you in the beat of a pigeon's wings that it was for Lacey Road.

Obviously the internet could have told you that too, but that's not nearly as impressive. In fact, to understand quite how impressive this is, one needs to understand that our sorting office oversees no fewer than 1,820 postcodes. I struggle to remember my own sometimes, so the fact that there are posties who possess these supernatural postcode powers puts, in my opinion, their memory skills up there with the revered brains of London cab drivers and their famous Knowledge exam, where they must memorise every street name in London along with the quickest route to it.

Anyway, while Little Larry had to go and sit down to recover from the notion of a world without addresses, the topic was of keen interest to other posties nearby. It was in this way that the intricacies of a world in which the streets really did have no name, as Bono had imagined, became the topic of extended debate. Opinions were varied:

"Sounds like 'eaven to oi!"
"You ejit, nobody'd get 'em letters!"
"Gary never read 'em addresses anyway!"

In the end everyone was able to find common ground on how they felt about Bono, so that was something. For a few minutes everyone returned to their letters in our world in which the streets do have a name, before the radio was suddenly turned off and the boss called us up to one end of the office. As ever, this was met with a chorus of unhappy grumbling. All along the aisles letters were petulantly slapped down onto desks, hands found their way to pockets and we slowly assembled around the manager at the far end of the warehouse like naughty schoolchildren.

These announcements were fairly common, but also fairly dull and seldom positive. They were rarely about pay rises or improved working conditions, for example. Also, as nobody wished to be in the warehouse any longer than necessary, and these announcements stood stubbornly against such wishes, they were always met with suspicion and distaste. So up we shuffled and gathered around, and off the boss went on his important announcements.

In fairness, there was some good news. One of the posties – the one whose garish socks had provoked so much interest on my first day – had reached 20 years of service with Royal Mail, and he was rightly recognised for such a feat. We clapped and hollered for him as he received what looked like a box with a medal in it. He started rifling through it as though looking for something else, and as we were all watching him we shouted that it wouldn't likely contain any money and that he'd have to do some work to earn some of that. He looked up, grinned wryly and went back to sitting on boxes of letters. The boss continued, and prattled on about this and that for a while, before dismissing us back to our sorting. As we shuffled away there were lots of funny comments about 20 years of service and only two years of work just loud enough so that the garish sock postie could hear, and so he yelled back gleefully and then that got everyone going: jibing and laughing, back and forth.

In the announcement there was a vague statement made about the concerns of that virus outbreak in China, and there were some nondescript assurances of workers' safety and remaining vigilant. One of the posties pointed out it was difficult to be vigilant about stuff you couldn't see. The boss agreed with that and he was palpably pleased that this allowed him to seamlessly slide into a warning about ice out on the roads. It had been a very cold night.

"Why's 'e warnin' us about ice for?" Big Barry muttered behind me, "'ow does 'e think we all got 'ere this morning?"

Some of the posties lived close enough to the sorting

office to walk to work, but many drove, and a few others cycled like me. Whatever one's mode of transport, though, the risk of ice would have been eminently obvious to anybody stepping out of their front doors this morning. It is laughable that Royal Mail force their managers to waste their time wasting postie's time with warnings that would only be effective if the company also supplied us with an alarm clock with all the hazards that the day ahead may or may not hold.

"Probably thinks we used teleportation, Barry" mused Little Larry. *Teleportation* said with a thick Bristolian accent, as it goes, is particularly pleasing to the ear.

Posties don't like being interrupted when they're sorting in the mornings, unless it's for good stuff, like cake, or a pay rise, or a strike maybe. There were growing murmurings of a strike, but the boss hadn't alluded to it. The Christmas just gone Royal Mail was supposed to strike, but it handily found a way to make it illegal so the union had to call it off. But another ballot has just voted heavily in favour of industrial action again and that's been getting everyone going once more.

Have you seen the forecast? There's a cold snap coming. Supposed to be worse than last winter. There's even talk of a few posties wearing trousers.

Frozen wishes,

P.

P.S. Apparently we've got eight cases of that virus in the UK now. I mean, it's not so surprising in a globalised world, is it? The cases are going up and up in China, but they say the risk is still 'moderate' here. We must have a good idea of how to handle it.

LETTER NINE

27th February

"February made oi shiver!
With every paper oi delivered!"

Or so sang the office this morning, as I pushed through the swinging doors. Appropriately so, too, given I had just cycled through falling snow to get there and I was most certainly shivering.

'American Pie' by Don Mclean was playing on the radio and it had the posties in fine spirits. Russell tended to be the lead on most songs, the postie who had been singing along to Bob Marley on my first day with Patricia. He's quickly become one of my favourite of the bunch. A round chap as wide as he is tall and as quick-witted as he is quick at sorting the post (that is, very quick), Russell was really giving his lungs over to it in his thick Bristolian accent.

"That'll be the day that I doy!"

The office inhaled as one and then:

"Sooo boye-boye Miss 'mericon poi!"

And so they went. After it was over, one of the posties asked, "When be a good toime to doy then, Russ?"

Russell looked at him straight in the eyes, "'Bout four o'clock?"

"Four o'clock is it?" The other postie was slightly taken aback, "That's not quite what I–"

"Yep, 'bout four o'clock," Russell nodded into the middle distance, "just after me missus brings oi tea."

And with that he went back to sorting his letters.

"February made oi shiver." These winds from the east are bringing a truly frightening freeze to our rounds. It's cold enough that the first letterboxes I come to each morning have frozen shut overnight, and I have to prise them open and risk catching my fingers on the stubbornest of them. There's nothing worse than hurting your fingers first thing in the morning – you feel it for every bit of post for the rest of the day and sometimes into the day after too.

"Bad news on the doorstep," Don sang next. It makes me wonder how much bad news I bring to people. The number of times I've heard, "If it's bills, you can take it back!" I have a well-practised chuckle to this one. But I hope that bills are – for the most part – the worst news I come bearing.

The biting air of Bristol is so cold that the atmosphere feels thick with tiny ice particles snapping at my bare skin like dogs' teeth, and infiltrating every layer of my clothing, of which I wear many. Despite the freezing conditions – and I really don't know how to explain this – I still happily wore shorts today. I needed four good layers on my top half, but my legs scarcely registered that they were exposed. The mystery of posties in shorts remains as baffling to me now as it did years ago, when being one myself had never entered my imagination.

The roads were jet black with ice against the snow-topped houses and hedges of the city. A fine crystal mist clung to the air and the low-arcing sun looked like a pale moon through the thick, cold haze above. A few chimneys sighed out the smoke of wood fires already burning inside, and even at mid-morning very few people had ventured out into the day. If you could even call it day, for it seemed more like some sort of white dusk, and it wasn't clear whether the temperature was supposed to go up or down from here. The streets, therefore, were mostly empty save for our army of red workers, wrestling with frozen letterboxes and cracking the skin of our cold knuckles as we knocked on cold doors.

The variation of receptions I receive when knocking on doors is quite extraordinary, ranging from delight to despair to downright confusion.

The delighted ones are the best, of course, and sometimes in gratitude these kind people ask me if I want anything to drink, or even if I need to use the loo. (While it requires putting a bit of faith in them, as far as I am concerned there is nothing more thoughtful in the world than offering up your toilet for a postie's use, who otherwise is at risk of spending half their working day trying not to disgrace themselves.)

I made a man particularly delighted today by delivering him a striking envelope, which he quickly explained to me was from the Queen for his 100th birthday. I had to blink a few times for it scarcely seemed plausible that this man was a century old. I wished him a happy birthday and many congratulations for getting this far, before politely shooing him back into his house, certain that the Arctic temperatures weren't going to be congenial to him making it a lot further. Then again, who am I to tell a centurion how to live?

The despairing customers, on the other hand, tend to be the ones doing the shooing. Just last week an old man came to his door and I asked him how he was. "Old and miserable," he replied laconically, and he took his parcel and smartly dismissed me with the close of a door.

The downright confused are the most amusing – and I'm sure they're often the result of drunk online shopping, for some people clearly aren't expecting the parcel I hand them. Sometimes, if you look closely enough into their searching eyes, you can see the memory of the late night, alcohol-induced shopping spree playing in their irises. A particularly memorable delivery of this nature was one I made to a Welsh lady who I think might be mildly but pleasantly inebriated most of the time, because she never really knows what she has or hasn't ordered, and seems to take great joy in saying outrageous things. Recently I handed her a book-shaped parcel, to which she responded in her thick Welsh accent, "But this is too thin to be my vibrator!" I wasn't quite sure how to reply to that.

Burn after reading,

P.

P.S. I'm sure you've seen the news about not getting too close to one another at the moment. Social distancing I think is what they're calling it. The posties had some fun with that when The Police came on the radio this morning:

"Don't stand so! Don't stand so! Don't stand so close to oi!"
Do stay safe though.

LETTER TEN

10th March

A westerly wind whisked me across wet streets to work this morning, as I joined the low-gliding seagulls soaring effortlessly on a tailwind around Bristol's harbour. I am invariably full of energy at this time of day – a happy accident when adapting to postie life – much like the seagulls of the city centre. They are most certainly awake too, and the shrieks of the night revellers have been replaced by those of these equally loud and populous animals, who take great joy in swooping down on overflowing bins, dropped boxes of chips and, occasionally, cycling posties.

Everything about Bristol suggests seaside town. Perhaps it's the prevailing southwesterly wind that whips through the city most days, bringing salty air in from the Atlantic and threatening to blow a postie's hat off their head as I find it funnelling around a corner. The seagulls add to this seaside sense too, of course, as do the pastel-coloured houses and the expansive harbour with all of the ships lining up around it.

The only thing is – and it's just a minor detail – there is a distinct lack of sea. The closest bit of sea is in fact six miles away – and that's as the crow flies. Even then it isn't really sea, but rather the muddy Severn Estuary that sucks and spits the water up and down the River Avon each day.

As I skirted my wheels around the wet cobbles of the harbourside, I found myself delighted at the morning light that March has brought to my commute. It is almost overwhelming quite how much happiness our emergence from the dark days of winter is bringing me. Indeed, it is so pleasant to find a hint of spring in the day that I have immediately forgiven all of winter and am decidedly glad that I live in this seasonal part of the world.

A glance over my shoulder, however, alerted me to an ominous black cloud closing in on the city with the wind. I pedalled harder, for there is nothing worse than a drenching before I've even got to the warehouse, where I will then have to stand damp and cold for hours as I sort my frame.

I made it just in time. As I pushed through the sorting office doors, the heavens opened above. The noise of torrential rain on the warehouse roof was a noise to be reckoned with, though it was nothing in comparison to the sound that it inspired from the posties. As the pitter-patter escalated to a thunderous drumming across the ceiling, the posties' grumbles increased to that of a synchronised roar. Quickly their voices were one: tribal cries pointed down at the letters they were sorting, but directed up at the heavens they were goading. Like apes in a cage, they were boisterous and booming, as if saying: 'Bring it on!' They've seen many days like it before and they'll see many more yet.

As the posties roared and the rain poured, managers ran around with buckets. The running joke was that the roof had more holes in it than Royal Mail's plan for the future, and to see the management scampering from one internal downpour to the next seemed rather befitting of current affairs in the company.

For the first time in a decade, the possibility of industrial action looms as large as the black cloud that deposited itself on the warehouse roof this morning. I mentioned that the trade union had organised for a strike to be held in the days building up to Christmas just gone, but Royal Mail successfully took it to the high court and got it stopped. Despite 110,000 postal workers voting in favour of a strike, Royal Mail argued that the union had interfered with the ballot by pressuring posties to vote in favour of it. This is baffling, to say the least. Of the seventy-six per cent of workers who had voted, ninety-seven per cent of them had voted to strike. Dictators around the world don't even bother to proclaim such convincing results in their so-called elections, and here was the British high court suggesting that a bunch of scruffy union members had managed to subvert the ballot with an almost Maoist efficiency. So there was to be no strike at Christmas, but with a watertight ballot in place the union says we are now ready to strike again. I hope the managers have got enough buckets.

Wishing you well from the toilet seat,

P.

P.S. People have started wearing masks in the warehouse. It's a strange thing: you can't really hear what they're saying and you don't know if they're smiling or not. But you can see the fear in their eyes if you accidentally get a bit too close to them. Now the virus has taken a hold in Italy, it suddenly feels like we might be in trouble. You hear people talking about it like an approaching tsunami... but what if it's already here?

A BRACE OF SHORT MISSIVES
ON FAILING TO PLEASE
EVERYONE

Dear Porch Owner,

Please forgive the postie yesterday who left your delivery in your porch. It probably seemed, to their mind, best for all concerned.

Yours apologetically,

P.

Dear Porch Owner,

Please forgive the postie yesterday who did not leave your parcel in your porch. It probably seemed, to their mind, best for all concerned.

Yours apologetically,

P.

❧ II ❧
SPRING

Satchel on hip
the postman goes
from doorstep to doorstep
and stooping sows
each letterbox
with seed. His right
hand all the morning makes
the same half circle. White
seed he scatters,
a fistful of
featureless letters
pregnant with ruin or love...

'The Postman', Jon Stallworthy

LETTER ELEVEN

21st March

Some years spring unravels itself gradually, as though an old coil prising slowly apart, or a newborn baby reluctantly opening its eyes to relinquish its cosy hibernation. Slow springs such as these are one harmonious and gentle awakening, but this is not at all what has happened this year. No, this spring has thrust itself upon us, shooting out of winter like an envelope through a letterbox.

I was walking up a garden path this morning and I heard it arrive. At first I thought it was the crack of the letterbox as it snapped shut, but on turning around to return down the garden path I saw that something else altogether had been delivered. No longer was the flower bed a mess of brown and nor were the trees bare and raw, but rather everything was suddenly greens and yellows and pinks. I had walked up the path in winter and, with the crack of a letterbox, the spring had sprung behind me as quickly and colourfully as a party popper pops. I have never known a season to arrive quite like it, but then perhaps I have just not been paying enough attention. If there's one thing being a postie does, it makes you acutely aware of what is going on outside, and it gives me the utmost pleasure to spend my days walking around in such unfolding glory.

If you are having a bad day in this job, there is no hope for you. A bad start will only mean that things get worse, for you start to rush and be hasty, make bad decisions and tie yourself up in knots. But the good days? My goodness, the good days are fantastic days, and one feels as though they are bouncing across a carpet of fallen blossom to the symphony of spring. My jubilance is partly explained by the arrival of this splendid season and partly by me having been put on a particular round in the absence of another postie. That postie is having an operation on his leg; this is not in the least surprising in the case of the old timers, because they've walked around Bristol for more days than I've been walking at all. Anyway, I've lucked out and will be taking his round on for a few weeks while he recovers.

His walk is based in Whitchurch, a delightful suburb of Bristol on the very fringe of the city to the point where one could almost call it rural. I even get to deliver to a farmer, who is a very friendly man with a very red nose, though even if he were unfriendly and his nose were not very red I wouldn't hold it against him. It is simply delightful to be out in the fresh air of the almost countryside, away from the mayhem and the fumes, where blossom floats from the trees like pink snow, the hum of the city has been replaced by the songs of the birds and the sweet smell of earth is tinged only occasionally by farm-induced aromas.

With every new street I delivered to today, spring followed me. I'd turn a corner, and the trees and the gardens would erupt into colour. I'd dart down a country lane and the bleating of newborn lambs came like a symphony over the hedgerows. I'd graze my leg against the vegetation of the bowered banksides only for the smell of wild garlic to gush through the air. I started to wonder if I had discovered my superpower, if in fact I was the bringer of spring, or if perhaps the satchel over my shoulder was packed not only with letters but with the seeds of a new season. Either way, today, I considered myself a new superhero. Today I was Springman.

Among all this joy there is one thing that is putting me off Whitchurch. It appears I am being mocked by one of the houses. There is a bungalow up in the corner of a small cul-de-sac that backs onto fields, where it is very quiet and there are never any signs that anybody is home. Sometimes I wonder if anybody lives there at all, until I am turning to go and it happens.

It is always just as I have posted the mail through the letterbox and taken two steps (no more, no less) away from the door, when a loud and shameless wolf whistle comes from inside the house. It is not timid by any account. Scaffolders would be proud of it, if they could pick their jaws up from the floor to purse their lips together to whistle at some poor woman walking by. Yes, it is a full-on *phhuuwwweeeeeet-phheeeew!* and I hardly know what to do with myself each time it occurs. I might be flattered if I wasn't so startled and confused.

All out of sorts,

P.

P.S. The penny has finally dropped for me about this coronavirus stuff and if I think about it too much I feel sick to the stomach. Ten *thousand* dead? The PM has said we should only go places if we have to. Why did we think we were so special as to avoid this?

LETTER TWELVE

I arrived at my frame at 6.30am, as I do every morning. I planted my feet squarely in front of it, took a deep breath and assessed the situation. Boxes of post and bags of parcels were already waiting for me: a thousand letters and hundreds of parcels, eager to be sorted into order. At this point a postie can already tell what kind of day lies ahead – and I knew I was on for a busy one. Maybe it was the look of worry on the manager's face, maybe it was something in the air, maybe it was simply that there was an inconceivable amount of stuff on my frame.

I set to work. While the frame is empty I like to get the door-to-doors in first, or junk mail as you'll know it. No doubt you dislike all this wasted paper, but rest assured that posties despise it far more than you do. Door-to-doors are fiddly to handle and we know they're destined for the bin. So I like to get them out the way by putting them in their allotted slots and not thinking about them again for a few hours, until I am trying to persuade them through uncooperative letterboxes. Don't tell anyone, but on days when I know I am passing an inconspicuous recycling bin on my round, I simply put all of the door-to-doors in there. It saves everyone a lot of time.

Next into the frame is the sequenced letters: those that a machine in Bristol's main sorting centre has been steadily arranging into order for us overnight. I've never seen one of these machines, but if I get the chance I might ask one of them to marry me, they're that fantastic. By some wizardry they are able to put the letters in the order that we deliver them on our round, so they're really easy to put into the right place on the frame. My hands can race along the rows popping them in their slots, one after the other, as quick as you like. Oh yes, those machines are wonderful things.

Then come the non-sequenced letters – those letters that the machine has not sorted into order for me – and this is the dreaded moment of the morning where the thinking has to begin. Having wandered warily over to the letter sorters section and snatched my walk's post from my pigeon hole, I then heave great boxes of these unordered envelopes back to my frame. Once there I scatter them across my desk and set about putting them in their slots. If you were on a frame you knew well, there was a satisfaction to how quickly you could do this. Your arms would fly back and forth from letter to slot to letter to slot, as your feet danced along the length of the desk. At times you don't even have to think about it: you just do it, with flying arms, dancing feet and a peaceful mind. It could be a meditation of sorts, if you let it. On the other hand, if you don't know where the addresses are on the frame, it can be a painfully slow process from which you emerge three hours later to find you have a throbbing headache and the warehouse is empty because everyone is already out on their rounds.

Then the parcels. Some days there are four or five big

bags, maybe more. The frames weren't designed with this number of parcels in mind – the frames are still a relic of the old days when Royal Mail specialised in mail – and so you have to do what you can to put the parcels in a sensible, logical place. There are various techniques: stand wobbling on the desk to balance each new parcel precariously atop the last; make a pile on the floor and risk it being kicked by another desperate and hasty postie; or just throw it on your York and hope you remember it when you are loading the van. Everybody is different, but nobody has a good solution when the parcels are coming thick and fast and there's no space to put them.

This prepping process takes hours. On bad days it can be four hours before you leave the sorting office. On bad rounds, that can be normal. On these bad days or on these bad rounds, I remind myself that there used to be a time when all this sorting was done on the night trains as they rolled out of London to the outposts around the country. In windowless, stuffy carriages, with no seating or proper sanitation, workers would sort post as they rumbled through the night. At least, I console myself, I could go to the loo.

Anyway, there are plenty of mornings when it takes me closer to two or three hours to prep the post, and these are more enjoyable. You can stand back once it is done and see how you have turned chaos into order. There is something beautiful about an organised frame that it is hard to describe to non-posties. In fact, it would be hard to describe it to a lot of posties themselves, for not all of them enjoy the order and discipline of sorting a frame. At least in their case they are spared the small but daily heartbreak of the moment when one's frame reaches the height of beautiful organisation, as this is also the moment in which it must all be taken down.

In some Eastern philosophies, and a few Western ones too, there is something known as the practice of non-attachment. That is, to be able to emotionally disengage with things in the world so as to not be overwhelmed. Many wise people practise this throughout their day, to train themselves for the truly terrible things that happen in their lives. To have to disassemble this orderliness every day by shoving the letters and parcels into a red satchel... well, I think it's as good a practice of non-attachment as any. And one that I often think about as I set about destroying my exquisitely arranged frame at around 9am every morning.

Namaste,

P.

P.S. No doubt you saw the news last night. Three-week lockdown. I'm not sure I even know what that means? I suspect our strike is off the table though.

LETTER FOURTEEN

29th March

Time is a tricky thing at the best of, well, times. But when it jumps about it can be really quite difficult to get your head around. I'm sure you went to bed on Saturday evening acutely aware that Daylight Saving Time was taking an hour of sleep away from you. A cause for grumbling no doubt, but – as everybody quickly remembers hot on the heels of that thought – at least there is the compensation of an extra hour of evening light going forward.

Well, one of our posties made it right through the weekend blissfully unaware of the changing of the clocks. Remarkable really, given even our phones know it happens and display the correct time without us needing to touch them. Perhaps he just goes by the time on his oven or still lives in the analogue world, because he had no idea the clocks had sprung forward an hour and so arrived to the sorting office an hour late this morning.

As you might imagine, he got some flak for it across the office. It was with great glee that the posties greeted the twangy strums of Bob Dylan coming on the radio, as 'The Times They Are A-Changin'' rang out across the floor.

"Yer song's on Gary!"

"Gary, have ye got the toime?"

"Watch out for them changin' toimes Gar!"

They all piled into him and piled their voices into the song. It started with those at one end of the warehouse, but come the final lyrics the whole workforce was in full voice, roaring at poor hapless Gary:

"And the first one now,
Will later be last,
For the times they are a-changin'!"

"Yer song's finished Gary!"

The clocks skipping forward an hour once a year is one thing, but house numbers skipping forward unexpectedly is a far more common trip hazard for posties. Specifically, skipping from number twelve to fourteen.

Understandably, people are a bit peeved when they receive the wrong post. If they're receiving their neighbour's bills, then they have reason to believe that maybe their letter about the doctor's appointment, or worse, that discreet item they're expecting has, in turn, accidentally gone to another neighbour.

We are not trying to get this wrong. It's just that there are so many ways in which it could go wrong, and so many letters to be delivered, that it is inevitable it sometimes does. Letters, for example, have an annoying habit of sticking together, which is why sometimes Mrs Smith at number five might also get Mrs Jones' post at number seven. Or, if there are no letters for anyone between Mrs Smith and Mrs Singh all the way along in number fifteen, then Mrs Smith's post might include a letter for Mrs Singh, even though she lives

100 metres down the road. It's an accident waiting to happen every day and at every stage of the process. Sometimes it really goes wrong and two letters posted in Warwick, say, stick together throughout the whole sorting process, and as a result a letter for someone in Wrexham turns up in Wigan.

We can't always blame the letters for sticking together, though. Quite often it is simply a postie's lack of concentration that lets it happen. During my first month I got halfway down Whitecross Avenue before I realised it wasn't Whitecross Avenue at all, but in fact the road it intersects with called Woodleigh Gardens. I turned around to grimace hard at the street I had just posted letters to, and gaze forlornly at the crossroads in the distance that I had walked the wrong way from. As I did so a lady stormed out of her house in her dressing down, a look of positive anger penetrating out of tired eyes and frazzled hair, having clearly just woken up – and woken up to the wrong post at that.

So, it happens. As I say, posties are not doing it deliberately, and I understand the frustrations people have, but we are mere humans and we make mistakes. While Royal Mail pay lip service to the fact that mistakes are inevitable, they seem determined to make them more likely in their actions: as the amount of work piles up for each postie every year, they are in more of a rush, and are more likely to give Mr James's doctor note to Miss Ashley, and Miss Ashley's latest discreet item to Mr James.

One area in which I will not concede the posties are to blame, however, is the case in which the house number skips from twelve to fourteen. You may not have heard of this, and neither had I before it became necessary for me to know it, but it turns out the superstition surrounding the number thirteen penetrates as deep into our society as the numbering of houses down a street.

The postie with their head down and rushing along to get

the letters delivered can easily miss the fact that number thirteen is missing on a given road. Property developers are now choosing not to have a number thirteen because it is harder and less profitable to sell, such is the profound stupidity with which our society has been gripped by the idea of unlucky number thirteen. I find consolation, at least, in the fact that other countries are just as moronic. In the USA, for example, skyscrapers often omit a thirteenth floor (I suspect we inherited such stupidity from them), while in Japan hotels, hospitals and apartment blocks often skip their unlucky number four. Meanwhile, back in England, the London Eye has thirty-two capsules but they are numbered up to thirty-three. Why? Yup, no number thirteen.

Indeed, the biannual hazard of changing clocks is nothing in comparison to the daily danger of number fifteen getting number fourteen's post, on account of number thirteen having never been built.

Inconsequentially,

P.

P.S. Speaking of house numbers, I'm starting to wonder if number ten Downing Street doesn't actually have a plan in place for the arrival of a deadly and contagious disease? Surely this routine science-fiction plotline has been given at least some thought by the upper echelons of the government before this moment? Because from this distance, it doesn't much look like it…

LETTER FIFTEEN

32nd March

Gary is the most unlucky postie in all of Bristol. Perhaps even in all of England. There's something about him that attracts trouble. His mere presence puts dogs across entire housing estates on edge; you can guarantee that whichever walk he is doing that day will be the heaviest walk in the office; and the managers treat him with an unfounded suspicion such that the slightest misdemeanour leads to a disciplinary. And, as we have seen, his clocks don't change while the rest of the country's do.

Even the letters rebel against Gary. More than once, he explained morosely to me, he's posted a letter through the letterbox, only to see it shoot back out from under the door and land at his feet. The only explanation for it is that the posted letter has arced perfectly downwards and slipped through the crack under the door. The odds of it happening to anyone seem slimmer than the breadth of a letter: the fact that it's happened to him more than once tells you all you need to know about Gary.

Gary turned up late to work again this morning. He slept through his alarm, he said. He was supposed to be helping out the posties who start sorting the unsequenced letters at some ludicrously early hour, so his tardiness was not only noticed but also despised. It was a particularly heavy morning for post, and sorting these unsequenced letters into their walks is a hard job. One has to be able to look at the road name and quickly recall which walk it's on: Wick Road... that's Walk Forty-One; Stoneleigh Crescent... that's Walk Forty-Nine... Knowle Road... that's Walk Fifty-Three. And so on, for thousands of letters, for hundreds of streets, for dozens of walks. So when Gary did eventually arrive, they let him know about it. There was ironic cheering and clapping, and even if you weren't anywhere near where they sorted the unsequenced letters in the office, you still joined in because that's the way it is.

Gary kept his head down and tried to make up for lost time, but he was the butt of all attention now and he wouldn't be left alone for the rest of the day. When Van Morrison's 'Brown Eyed Girl' came on the radio with its unmistakable intro, the posties found new lyrics for it:

"Hey, where did Gary go?
Days when he's so late!"

Sha-la-la-la-la-la-la-la-la-la-la-te-da rang through Gary's ears for the rest of the day, no doubt.

I saw an interesting article in the paper the other day about an ex-professional goalkeeper. David Harvey played for Scotland and Leeds some years ago before going on to become a postie. He talked lovingly of the sorting office, and how it was just like the football dressing rooms he had spent the past few decades in. I have described to you the wit and the commotion across the warehouse floor and the tribal cries that come out when the rain pours down, and I can't think of a more apt comparison than that which David Harvey observes.

Pranks are never too far away from a dressing room, and Gary – if he wasn't already – made himself the target of them this morning. This conversation might amuse you:

"What's the date?" Gary asked, once the unsequenced was finally sorted, and he was filling out a form.

"March 32nd, Gar."

"Right," said Gary, and he started writing down March 32nd on the document. Well, obviously those around him leapt quickly into laughter.

"What?" Gary looked up, bemused.

"Nothing at all, Gar, nothing at all," they said, "Happy March 32nd to you!"

Not long after that Gary realised it was, in fact, April 1st. He smiled, closed his eyes and shook his head. He was a good sport was our Gary, and he knew he'd been got good. But they had plenty left in store for him this morning, from hiding his bags of parcels, to barricading his desk with dozens of empty boxes, to even getting Bert in on the act.

Gary had been queuing up for his 'specials' like the rest of us, and when he got to the front of the queue Bert informed him that he had forty-six items to sign for and deliver. The most specials Gary had ever heard anyone receiving was nineteen and that's awful enough in itself. At the idea of forty-six specials Gary descended into a hissy fit befitting of a playground, much to the amusement of all those around, most of all Bert, who in the meantime had placed Gary's two specials on the desk and was waiting there gleefully and patiently with a pen in his outstretched hand for Gary to sign for them. When Gary noticed, he smiled, closed his eyes and shook his head. Trademark Gary, that is. He's an unlucky sod, but I like him.

As for myself, I got out of the office at a decent hour today and went about my rounds in Whitchurch. I had a good day – certainly better than Gary's day in any case – but I did get wolf whistled at again. The moment of the wolf whistle is so punctual that I have to assume this person is waiting for me so they can emit it. But the time at which I arrive to the house each day can vary by several hours depending on what order I decide to do the route, and it seems too mad to entertain the idea that somebody is waiting all hours of the day to wolf whistle at their postman.

It is baffling, but the reality is I am too busy to give it more than a few seconds thought each day. My hands have already started to occupy themselves with flipping through all the letters for the next house and before I know it I'm off and away down the cul-de-sac.

Disconcertedly,

P.

P.S All this amid a pandemic that we haven't quite got our heads around yet. It's weird and it's scary. Even the radio DJs have been thrown off and can't stop playing 'It's the End of the World as We Know It' by REM. It turns out no other pop song quite captures the dystopia like this one does.

A SHORT MISSIVE ON DOGS
IN GARDENS

Dear Dog Owner,

Your dog was loose in your garden and so I couldn't deliver you your letters today. I had no other means of getting in touch with you to let you know, so I wrote it in a book in case you checked here.

With all fingers intact,

P.

LETTER SIXTEEN

17th April

As I pedal my way to work, the hush on the streets of Bristol reliably makes amends for the pain of the alarm clock. A reason to get out of bed is all we can really ask for, and often – no matter what is to come in the ensuing hours – that fifteen minutes of cycling across the city makes my day. The Bristol drizzle is a lotion to a tired face, the task of pedalling gratifying to stiff muscles and there lingers an irrepressible beauty in this quiet solitude.

My commute contrasts starkly to that of the mayhem I invariably find as I push through the sorting office doors. No matter what the weather in the given moment I stepped out of my front door, the atmosphere of the sorting office at 6.30am always slaps harder in the face. Trolleys crashing, radio blaring, posties shouting.

If one likes to be with one's thoughts for a little while at the start of the day, the chaos can take a bit of getting used to. What's funny, though, is that – despite the dressing-room feeling that David Harvey so poignantly described – this can still be the loneliest of jobs. Indeed, for many it is. This system is such that one doesn't need to utter a word all day, if one doesn't want to. Putting the letters and parcels into the frame could be a seamless and solo process, and many a morning has passed where postmen and women have passed in and then out of the swinging doors without uttering so much as a grunt or groan. It's incredible that one could do such a job in total silence really, but the processes are so heavily engrained that there is actually very little need for talking. It's like we are all machines, robotically going about our work. Inevitably, therefore, this means that almost all of the talking is nonsense. Delightful nonsense perhaps, but nonsense no less.

As amusing as those first few hours of the day are, it is also a relief to push my York out of the doors and to go blinking into the day, where I can study how it has changed during my hours under the fluorescent lights. I transfer the load from my York to my van, sometimes with a meticulousness that would bore an accountant, sometimes with a haphazardness that would give them a heart attack. It depends how I feel.

This morning, once the van was full, I paused for a brief moment to behold the volume of things within it. It was baffling that I'd be returning here at some point – likely once the sun had dipped back below the horizon again – and the van would be empty. How, I asked myself as I stared despondently at my work for the day, would I deliver all of this? Well, much like writing a book perhaps: one letter at a time. This was just another task that had to be chipped away at: letter by letter, step by step.

There is one more very important thing still to be done before heading out on the round: to seize the last chance to relieve oneself before a day out on the streets. Often I arrive at the urinals at the same time as Arthur, an amiable and talkative postie, who I always seem to be on the same schedule as, in all senses of the word. We stand there silently facing the wall, which I am quite comfortable with, although I can sense he is not and he feels the need to say something. Invariably, after a few seconds he'll let out a sigh and declare:

"They say there's seventy-three per cent chance of rain at ten o'clock…"

"Right," I'll say. Then Arthur will proceed to tell me all about the forecast for the rest of the day and I have to loiter in the corner listening so as not to be rude (Arthur's bladder's not what it once was), as frowning posties come and go.

It's a little peculiar, I'll grant you, but it is very useful to have a weather enthusiast accompany you at this interlude. As I walk back to my van I have an excellent idea of what time I should sit in it to eat my lunch as the heavens open and the loops on which I should take a waterproof, just in case.

The next few minutes are among my favourite in the day. As one drives down our road and into the city, it is probable that there are a few other posties going at the same time, for we are all on similar and often disarmingly precise timings. The thrill of a fleet of Royal Mail vans heading out across the city and countryside in unison, dispersing like busy red bees, is electric. It is what one imagines being part of an army might feel like: each of us being deployed to our posts, armed with purpose and a noble mission. I like to think of the thousands of red vans across the country that are also leaving their sorting offices at this very moment too. It is like taking a bird's eye view of the UK and seeing these red bees emerge from their hives to methodically pollinate the country with love, leaflets and… well… bills.

Perhaps then, in terms of a collective noun, a swarm of posties might be what we're after. I must admit though it seems a bit chaotic to me: a swarm is not befitting of the discipline of a system in which not a single word need be uttered over the course of a day. But then I have also often thought that posties, as well as being like bees, are somewhat like ants: we both emerge en masse from hidden nests and carry great weights on our backs for great distances. So, if an army of ants, perhaps an army of posties? No, I know what you're thinking: too aggressive. I agree.

Well, in any case, the infrastructure this institution has built is truly astonishing and all too easily taken for granted. What began as a way for a king to send his letters has resulted in an organisation that can reach every *single* house on six out of seven days of the week, all year round. That moment of the day when a fleet of red vans takes to the streets is another step towards that daily success, and yet it is such a common sight to the general public that it doesn't inspire so much as a blink.

Evidently (and admittedly rather sadly) I find this whole thing fascinating – and the excitement of our red vans dispersing across the city makes me want to toot my horn, although I'm not sure my enthusiasm would translate well this way. So I allow myself a big smile, turn up the radio and marvel at the curious amount of pride I have in being part of something so much bigger than myself.

May the good lord not mind thy presence on Earth,

P.

P.S. Another three weeks of lockdown? People are losing their minds indoors. But from those making the rules at the top, to those of us following the rules at the bottom, at least we're all in the same boat.

LETTER SEVENTEEN

30th April

The days are lengthening and the air is warming, but not all is improving. We posties are as busy as we were at Christmas, and I'm sure a strange mood has gripped the country. Just this morning I was delivering parcels around Whitchurch and a man shouted a four-letter word out of his bedroom window at me. I had parked in the only available space that, admittedly, was in front of his drive, but any sane person could have seen that I had a singular parcel and was bound for his neighbour's front door with it. The delivery would have taken me all of sixty seconds, and given he was sat looking forlornly out of his bedroom window it's not like he was going anywhere anytime soon. But, still, he swore at me and told me to move my van.

I do wonder what goes through people's heads when they speak to somebody like this. Perhaps not very much at all and that's why they do it. I cannot speak for them, but I can – to some extent – speak for posties and so I shall try to give you a glimpse into our heads now.

For the public, a postie is seemingly everywhere and nowhere at once. A mere glimpse of red coming to the front door, a quick shout of the letterbox and then gone again for another day. Gone for you, that is, but only so as to be arriving for somebody else.

What is it like to be this ever-present person on the street? What goes through a postie's head as they trundle along, from door to door, house to house? Each of us are different, of course. As Little Larry and Big Barry attest, posties come in all shapes and sizes, and one must assume that is true of our thoughts too.

Many are gregarious types who want to chat with everyone they see: adult or child, cat or dog, wind or wall. But these types have found their conversations are being seriously constrained by the increasing time pressure on our day. A private company doesn't want to waste time and money on something as inefficient as a *chat*. That was for the days when the taxpayer funded such things. But no longer, absolutely not.

It so happens that I am not the most gregarious anyway – and indeed there are more introverted posties than you might think. After the loud, rowdiness of the morning in the sorting office, it is a relief for me to step into the quiet of the streets and go about my business in the company of only my thoughts. For me, there is much satisfaction to be found in this productive solitude, and peace to be found in the physicality and discipline of posting.

Allow me to invite you into my head for the length of a road. Stepping out of the van at one end, I heave a satchel over my shoulder, nestle a bundle into my elbow and set off down the houses. My inner monologue goes something like this:

"Letter for number one, number three, number five and now a parcel for seven. Knock knock knock. Morning!

Cheers, thank you, no worries. She seemed grumpy. Next letter is for number nine, now eleven, now fifteen. Damn! I put that in number seventeen... Where is... ah... they skip number thirteen. Idiots. Knock knock knock. Hi, yep, sorry wrong house, won't happen again. Cor, they looked angry. Okay, let's put number seventeen in number seventeen's house – perfect, there we are. And now there's not another letter until halfway down the road, magic! So I can raise up my head, draw back my shoulders and take a moment to breathe it all in. The fresh morning air, the sun gleaming down, the budding flowers in the gardens. This is the bit of the day I live for, where I can take in Mother Nature and bask in her... Shit, I've walked past ten houses I should have delivered to. Right, back I go again. Concentrate, man. Oh, that's a nice butterfly. A red admiral, I believe. In fact I'm sure it is because it's the only butterfly I know. Ah, number thirty-one, here are your bills, lovely job. Thirty-three, thirty-five, thirty-seven. *Phhhhwwweeeeettt-Phhheeew!* Oh will you please cease your whistling!"

So it goes,

P.

P.S. The PM says we're past the peak now, maybe this nightmare will end soon? The world might have stood still, but the posties have been running faster every day, and it's taking its toll.

LETTER EIGHTEEN

11th May

"The firs' twenty-five years is the worst," the murderous, macho postman said to me this morning. "It gets a bit better after that."

It seems to me a fairly reliable rule that the longer one does something, the more adept one becomes at discovering all the things one hates about it. In a little over six months I already have quite the collection of pet peeves. I dread to think what that collection would look like after twenty-five years, although I suspect *stupid new posties who lose their special deliveries* is tucked away in a dusty corner somewhere.

The rain, you might be surprised to learn, is not among such pet peeves. I'm sure I'm not the first to point this out, but it is only water. I can understand that it's an annoyance if you have plans to go for a picnic, head to the beach, or just generally be outside and reposed. But we are outside and marching the streets, and – most days – we come prepared for what the weather is offering. Plus, when you have a weather forecaster stationed at the urinals, you can't go too far wrong.

Indeed, the rain is by no means the problem with this job. The clothes Royal Mail give us aren't bad, in fairness, so I stay mostly warm and dry. I wear shorts, of course, but when have you ever seen a postie not wearing shorts?

It's the wind that I can't stand. Too many days at sea in a previous life, perhaps. The rain doesn't try and take away my letters, but the wind sure does. Should a Bristol dweller have glanced out of their kitchen window on a windy day in recent months, they're sure to have spotted me running down the street in pursuit of an envelope that a wicked wind has whisked from my bundle. When the wind coincides with days where I've got a stack of flimsy leaflets – normally a Domino's pizza flyer or something else equally bin-worthy – then my day is destined to be bad. Trying to guide a flailing flyer through a stubborn letterbox is one of the most unexpectedly frustrating things I have ever had the misfortune to battle with, and the fact that I have to do it one hundred times on these windy days is salt in the wound.

Gates. That's another one that really gets to me. Gates. Most gates – I am certain – serve no purpose at all, other than to get in my way. The majority of housing in Bristol is terraced, and terraced houses have garden gates only one metre away from their front door, where they sit rusting and obstinate and doing absolutely nothing, save for slowing down the postie. A row of houses *without* gates can be posted to twice as quickly as a row of houses with them. I've noticed that gate care doesn't seem to rank very highly on people's agendas. Most gates I've come across have either faulty latches, broken hinges, rusting frames, or a combination of all of the above. There's one gate just down the road from that house that wolf whistles at me, which is in a state of such disrepair that I have to dismantle it every time I'm posting them a letter and then reassemble it again as I'm leaving. I'm genuinely considering bringing a toolkit to work with me to make the round a little quicker. This is a house, by the way, that recently put a 'Thumbs up for your postie' sticker on their front door. I see these around quite a bit and it's a nice gesture, but what would be a whole lot nicer than some sticker that only the postie actually sees, is if they were to fix their sodding gate! I don't like gates.

But there is one pet peeve of mine that ranks above all others. Numbers on doors. Or numbers *not* on doors, I should say. Why don't people have numbers on their doors? It's outrageous. It should be a crime. Make them post all the letters and parcels to their street for a week, I say. Let them see how practical it is when people don't have numbers on their doors. They'd argue that there are only a couple of dozen houses on the street, surely one would remember which house is which after a while? Well, perhaps, yes, but in my short time as a postman so far I have already been dispatched to hundreds of streets, and I'm buggered if I'm remembering the number of every house that has opted to make it a guessing game as to how far along the street you might be. I don't want to be too dramatic about this, but I honestly believe there might be a special place in hell reserved for those who do not have numbers on their doors.

Some people opt to number their bins – for it is apparently more important to number a bin than a house – and perhaps they think this redeems them. The problem with this, however, is that the bins that get wheeled out of one house on a given week, invariably get wheeled back into another for the bin collectors also don't know which house is which. Then the postie really hasn't got a clue which way is up and which way is down. *Then* there are those who choose to grow trees beneath their letterboxes, or perhaps hanging plants above them, and so one has to squeeze between the poorly placed wilderness to cram a letter through the hidden slot. Don't even get me started on Christmas wreaths.

As for houses that wolf whistle at you, well, I don't know what I can say about them, but I am beginning to feel harassed and don't know what to do about it. It's just the first twenty-five years that are bad, is it? Well, only another twenty-four and a half to go then.

May your gates be stolen in the night,

P.

LETTER NINETEEN

27th May

If the radio or TV people ever found themselves short of a weather presenter in the moments before they do their bit, they could do worse than go down to the street and grab the first postie they find. If they're really in a pickle then they can always find my friend in the urinals, who is sure to be telling the plumbing the percentages of precipitation for the ensuing hours.

I spend a disproportionate amount of time talking about the weather – even by British standards – so I really do think I could do that bit on the radio or TV. What I'd really like, though, is if they had a bit where someone talked about the seasons.

"What's the season up to today, Pat?"

"Well, Nick, it bein' late spring and tha', and as my friend from the urinals jus' explained, it's gonna be a real 'ot one today, so we'll see they spiders comin' out in droves."

"Spiders, you say?"

"Yeah, spiders. 'Ole clusters of 'em. An early 'eatwave like this

makes 'em all think it's Glastonbury Festival, and they pitch up
their webs everywhere and 'ave theyselves a party."

And that would be our daily season update. It's still news after all, isn't it? Just not the normal terrible news that we're used to hearing. It could be part of an effort to bring people's attention to the outside a little bit, rather than getting lost on the inside of their houses, office buildings or computer screens.

To be fair, news of spiders pitching up their webs across the country would not be considered as good news to many. Since one very hot day last week, it really has been quite astonishing how many cobwebs have appeared. It transpires that a favoured spot for spiders to set up camp is at the entrance to front gardens, just between the hedgerows. I have, therefore, spent much of the past week walking into them, for I am more often looking at the bundle of letters in my arms than at where I am going. The web collapses and wraps itself instantly around me, and so – quite naturally – I end up dancing around manically, partly to brush off the web, but mostly to rid myself of any potential bulging arachnid.

Several people have watched on from their front windows at this peculiar display and when they come to the door I have to explain that it's the cluster of spiders out on the streets. They look at me quizzically and I implore that it is true – they all came out after the hot day last week thinking it's Glastonbury Festival – but people only step back from the door and slowly close it, eyeing me suspiciously.

Spiders are hardly known for their social habits and yet a cluster of spiders is a relatively well-known collective term. I remain baffled that no such term has been extended to posties. Perhaps it is because the only time one sees more than a pair of posties together they are on the inside of a sorting office, and this is obviously hidden from public view. Indeed, the public have had over 500 years to become accustomed to the notion of the lone postie and so to see several in one place might be rather overwhelming. In part I think this is what makes postal strikes so unnerving. A picket line of posties might look as if a collection of otherwise single predators have banded together, like a group of leopards realising that if they work as one they might be more effective. And yet leopards are the most solitary big cat in the world, rarely seen together, but even they have a collective noun: a leap of leopards!

Many professions, in fact, have collective nouns even though you wouldn't presume to ever find them in groups. There's a drift of fishermen, a discretion of priests, a doctrine of doctors! There's even a sodom of shepherds and a worship of writers, and I can hardly think of two more solitary occupations in the world than a shepherd or a writer.

I must admit, I do wonder about the reliability of these collective nouns sometimes. They are often so bizarre and flamboyant (incidentally, a group of flamingos is known as a flamboyance) that they are surely made up. When it comes to language, though, it's all made up, isn't it? And my point is – whether the nerds behind the Oxford English Dictionary have sanctioned it or not – nobody in the world seems to have "made up" a collective noun for posties. They seem etymologically destined to spend their days alone, only ever to come together in defiant moments of industrial action, which serve to put everybody at unease for there is not even a word to describe such a gathering of people.

Perhaps if there were a word to describe this scant-seen group, it would be less daunting when they are found together. People are much more at ease with things when they can put a name to them, after all. But what would a collection of posties be? Actually, that's quite good: a collection of posties. We do collect these days. What do you think? Bit tacky, perhaps.

Collectively,

P.

P.S. Did you see about the PM's advisor driving the entire length of the country with his family during lockdown? Then they went for a sixty-mile drive on his wife's birthday to "test his eyesight to drive". They even reckon they had Covid. Perhaps we haven't all been in this together after all.

LETTER TWENTY

9th June

You are right. A good way to overcome all those silly pet peeves of mine is to remember the wider picture. It is so easy for us to get bogged down in the menial things, isn't it? There is a useful strategy I once heard about how to deal with situations when you find yourself going around in sad circles inside your head. It's very simple – and also very suitable for posties.

What you do is this. When you are trapped in your head and everything is going wrong, you consider yourself from above, as if from the perspective of a bird hovering just over your head. There you are: you and your thoughts. Then imagine the bird flying up a bit higher, and now the view is of you and those you live with. You are but one person going about your business – one bundle of letters wrapped up in a fleshy satchel – but others are also precisely that too, with their own bills to pay and letters of heartbreaking news to digest.

Let the imaginary bird soar higher and you will see your

neighbours along your street: all navigating the world in their own ways, dealing with their own stuff, entirely unaware of your struggles in that moment. Fly a little higher still and you see more streets, and the people in the park and the long lines of vehicles driven by people stuck not only in traffic jams, but also in their own heads. Higher and higher yet and you will see the whole postcode, the whole town, the whole county, full of people all dealing with their own complicated lives.

I've found this charming little exercise can be really quite powerful on those days when a flailing, flimsy flyer just won't get into that letterbox. All the angry letters that circle round and round in my head – with no delivery address and no real purpose – can be quickly dispersed by zooming out from myself and realising they're just as much junk mail as the thing in my hand. Both can be put in the bin.

So, indeed, the wider picture! You ask me to recall why I chose to become a postie and I think that it is the right question to ask myself at this juncture. It was for a number of reasons, all of them good ones I believe, though not all of them have turned out to be correct.

To work outside was very high up on my list. Well, the job has most certainly provided that and – rain or shine – I am very glad for it. I was not anticipating quite so many hours beneath the glaring lights of the sorting office each morning, that is true, but *c'est la vie*, as the French say.

The French have another useful word for describing my decision. 'To work' in French is *travailler*. Isn't it interesting that *travailler* has the same root as the English word, 'travel'? This can hardly be a coincidence. But then to travel *is* also to work, for no travel is taken without effort. But is it also the case the other way around? Is it that to work is to travel? Well, it certainly is for a postie. Indeed, work for me is to meet different folk, see new sights and smell the earth rising up from around the trees. If that isn't travel, I don't know what is.

I also thought being a postie meant being a part of something larger than myself. I thought it meant community, I thought it meant connecting people. I think a lot of people still consider this to be the role of the postie, and that this is why whenever I meet somebody new and they discover I am a postman they are delighted at the idea. Here is a citizen who links us all together, they think, who walks the bridges that connect everyone to anyone, regardless of who they are. To the people, we are the adhesive glue on the envelope: lick us and we bind you! (But please check first with your postie if they're happy to be licked.)

While I certainly do spend a gratifying amount of time outside and I do consider my job as a daily travel of sorts, this last reason for becoming a postie is harder to hold on to. It's hard to believe one is the glue that brings everyone together when there is so much moving people apart. As we are learning, an entire population can stay in their house and be brought what they need to survive. They can spend time with their families through the internet and never have to go to the shops because the shops come to them nowadays. Or rather, delivery people come to them.

Far from bringing people together, I am starting to wonder if being a postie actually means bringing people either the bills they claim to not be able to afford, or the endless stream of material items that they very much seem able to afford. It is a disheartening realisation and it rather makes me question what the postie in the modern world is ultimately for.

Certainly for that bungalow at the top of the cul-de-sac, the postie remains for wolf whistling at. A sharp *Phhu-uwwweeeeeet-Phheeeew!* rings like an alarm every time I step back from the door. I've half a mind not to deliver there at all and let the postie who covers it on my day off take a week's worth of post to this strange place.

The badgers fly at dawn,

P.

A SHORT MISSIVE ON THE
MYSTERY OF THE WOLF
WHISTLE

Dear Resident at Number Thirty-Seven,

Your postie that normally covers Whitchurch came back to work after his knee operation and we had a chat. I asked how he was getting on and he told me he'd had an operation on his knee and I said I know, that's what I meant. He said it was alright and he was pleased to be moving again. He asked how I'd got on and I said pretty good, it had been nice to be out near the countryside.

Then he asked me what I thought of the parrot at number thirty-seven and I said what parrot is that then. The parrot in the bungalow, he looked at me bemused, surely you heard it. The thing whistles every time I go there, he said.

I looked at him stupidly for a few moments and he asked if I was alright. I said, what the bungalow? He said, yeah, I said the bungalow. I said, the bungalow at the top of the cul-de-sac? Yep, he said. Then I said, the bungalow at the top of the cul-de-sac where somebody wolf whistles at me every time I step back from the door? That's a parrot, he replied. THAT'S A PARROT?! I sort of shouted. He went a bit red, embarrassed for me. Well actually, he muttered, there's a few parrots I think. I stared stupidly for a bit longer and I don't think he knew what to say, so he said, I think they call it a company of parrots... when there's more than one, you know... a collective noun, or something.

I regained some composure and finally said sorry, it's just that I thought I was being harassed and now I find out it's been a company of parrots all this time.

Furiously,

P.

❧ III ❧
SUMMER

Nothing happened at all except summer.

'Cider with Rosie', Laurie Lee

LETTER TWENTY-ONE

21st June

One can be certain that summer has arrived to Bristol with just a glance to the heavens twice a day: once at dawn, once at dusk. In this small corner of the world, and at this time of year, the cerulean sky is as clear of clouds in the morning as the sorting office is of letters in the afternoon. But it is not just this impeccable clarity that speaks of summer, nor simply that Bristol is soaked in a golden hue, but the fact that these long days are invariably bookended by a colourful array of hot air balloons gliding across the sky.

This morning I heard them before I saw them. Bewitched as I was by the light scattering off the water in the harbour and by the warmth of the air as I cycled through it at that early hour, I had not yet thought to look up. But when the hot air balloon's flame came on the roar of it reached my ears in the city below. I immediately looked up because the first balloon of the summer is a moment, as they say, to write home about. This quick jerk upwards earned me a stomach-dropping swerve across the road and so quickly I looked ahead again. Steadying myself, I craned my neck up once more and saw the great basket and balloon only 100 metres above me, and I could see the pinhead-sized faces of its passengers. If it was a magnificent sight for me, I can only imagine how wonderful it would have been for them. It was the first of many balloons drifting over the city this morning, as if aerial posties coming to deliver the summer on a gentle westerly wind. (Incidentally, aerial posties may not be many years away, but they will come in the form of drones rather than hot air balloons, which I think is a great missed opportunity.)

It is the reliability of the wind direction that makes balloons such a common sight in Bristol's summer season. Launching from the fields across the iconic Clifton Suspension Bridge, the balloons rise up and catch the breeze over the city. The beauty of Bristol is that one is never too far away from fields on the other side of it, and as the balloons disappear to the eastern horizon one can be reasonably hopeful that the passengers will find a soft landing in a green meadow not too far away.

It has not escaped local artists' attention that the colours of the balloons in the summer sky nicely complement the pastel-coloured houses lining many of Bristol's hilltops. In seaside style, a given row of houses in Bristol is highly likely to be painted in alternating yellows, pinks and blues, and many an artwork can be found at the markets that attest to this tradition. The bright houses overlooking the harbour in the city centre are no doubt best known for this, but my favourite are to be found at the top of Totterdown's perilous hill. Silhouetted against the pink of the morning sky, they watch as dawn draws light to the city, entices hot air balloons to the sky and drags me to the sorting office nestled at the foot of their hill.

"I be runnin' up tha' road!
I be runnin' up tha' hill'
I be runnin' up tha' buildin'!"

A chorus of jubilant posties were simultaneously bastardising and Bristolising Kate Bush's lyrics as I entered the warehouse this morning. I wasn't the only one buoyed by the start of summer, it seemed. The endorphins the body delivers to us on these warm and bright mornings get unwrapped and spill out across the sorting office in a contagious manner, and apparently posties are to be found in the highest spirits as summer dawns.

That is, until a manager comes around and announces, "Don't forget your flex!", which in layman's terms means there's a walk that isn't being covered today and everyone has to take an extra bundle of letters from that frame to make sure it gets done. This is a surefire way of putting posties right back into a wintery mood, because now they have to do more work than they expected when they arrived an hour ago. So it goes.

Before long I really am running up the road, the hill and the buildings, as I charge about the streets trying to offload all the post for another day. The beauty of it, though, is that a time always comes when the van is empty. Then I can cycle home, put my feet up and not think about it again until my alarm early the next morning.

Full of hot air,

P.

P.S. They're easing the lockdown. After weeks of wishing it would all go away, I'm now, quite peculiarly, a bit worried that I might miss it. Do you know what I mean?

LETTER TWENTY-TWO

1st July

With the start of summer I have been moved to yet another walk. I will miss the rural life of Whitchurch; alas as a new postie I cannot pick and choose which walk I do. Some posties have to wait a decade or more before they are finally given the walk they want. Longevity and loyalty are, eventually, rewarded at Royal Mail.

The postie who has covered Walk Fifty-Three for the past few years has to have an operation on his ailing knee, and that tells you all you need to know about the summer that is ahead of me. He has walked in an increasingly hobbly fashion for some time now and there is no doubt in anybody's mind that this round had more than its fair share to do with it. Having done it in his absence once or twice before, I consider him nothing short of a hero. It is a truly ghastly round that gets a despicable amount of post and parcels even on the quietest of days, and while summer usually offers many such days this is clearly not a usual summer.

The first two roads of Walk Fifty-Three are long and the satchels are heavy, but the real problem is the vertiginous ascents one has to make to the houses built on the upper side of the road. Rows of terraced Edwardian houses were built into the hillside of Knowle and if you didn't have to post to each one of them you'd probably think they were quite pretty. As it is, to get to the front door a postie has to climb up a steep set of steps to reach each individual house and so I have long-stopped caring whether they are pretty or not. It is a leg-burning, back-bruising, morale-sapping start to the day – and that's after just the first three houses.

Indeed, the beginning of Walk Fifty-Three is, it has been commonly agreed, one of the worst in our postcode area. Things improve slightly after the hill has been ascended, although not by much, and soon enough that hillside climbs yet again, and therefore so does the unfortunate postie. Panting up and down the steps to each individual house along Rookery Road is a particularly loathsome way to spend thirty minutes of one's day, especially if the thirty minutes happen to fall on a hot summer's afternoon. Like today, as a matter of fact.

Nobody on Rookery Road minds if I nip between gaps in the hedge, or jump a wall perhaps, so as to avoid going all the way back down to street level each time. Nobody apart from the lady in the second to last house, who stormed out and reprimanded me for ducking under her metal railing and onto the neighbour's garden path, even though it was as harmless to her and her garden as a paper cut is to a rhinoceros. I stood there with sweat streaming down my face, heaving lungfuls of hot city air into me and stared blankly back at her. Some people just like to tell us what to do.

Then comes Wells Road. This is the A37, the main road bringing people into the city from the south. You can still picture the tranquil scene of horse and carriage riding down this road in the years before the city started to sprawl, and consider what a picture of serenity it would have been. Nowadays, it is hell on tarmac: lorries thunder in and out of the city; buses block up the lanes and blast their horns at everyone else; everyone else sits in their cars waiting patiently, until the opportunity to tear down the road arises and suddenly they're a sprint driver; and then cyclists and scooter riders suddenly appear between this medley of vehicles, ducking and weaving perilously down the hill.

I stand on the side of the road and watch this for a lot of the day. Not because I am lazy or because it interests me, but because at several parts of the loop I must wait to cross the road so that I can deliver back down the other side to where my van is parked. I have often stood at the side of the road for five minutes or more, unable to cross it without risk of death or moderate to serious injury. This might not seem like a long time, but if you have to do it six times – as one does when they are posting on Walk Fifty-Three – then that five minutes becomes thirty minutes, and that is a long time in the day of a postie. Each walk is supposed to be precisely calculated so that it takes roughly the same time as any other, but does this take into account the time it takes to cross Wells Road six times? Does it heck.

It is also, rather savagely, the road that all the other posties take to get back to the sorting office. So I watch them all returning at the end of their day as I stand on the side of the road with a satchel full of post and think how nice it must feel to be on the way home. At least the posties will likely see me and stop so that I can cross the damned road. They give me a meek smile and a nod, because they'll have done Walk Fifty-Three at some point in their long posting lives and they'll know the pain I am going through.

At the end of the day, when one finally gets back to the

office to find the gates locked and that everyone has already gone home, one starts to questions one's priorities in life. That being said, although Walk Fifty-Three is awful, I am pleased to know that I have my own walk for the time being. It is more preferable to me than to be shipped from pillar to post around the office, clearing up other people's work that they didn't finish the previous day. At least I am now in control of my own destiny, even if that destiny is to collapse in a heap at the end of each shift.

In support of zebra crossings,

P.

P.S. A zeal of zebras... a zeal of posties? No, you're right, we're not enthusiastic enough.

LETTER TWENTY-THREE

9th July

It is something of a travesty for the postie that although he or she gets to work outside for most of the day, there is seldom the opportunity to look around and take it all in. We are tracked and monitored and time is not our own. For the time that we are in our uniform we are as much a possession of the Royal Mail machinery as the letters that carry stamps, and rarely do we get the opportunity to enjoy the great outdoors in which we spend so much of our time.

Well, this morning I was having none of it and I stole back five minutes of time that is rightfully mine anyway. It was a summer's morning too splendid not to stop and breathe in.

I didn't realise it to begin with: I was on one of those ghastly steep roads I mentioned, the ones that make a postie's legs burn like the midday sun. But when I reached Bayham Road and parked on the corner of Lilymead Avenue, I stepped out of my van and what I saw stopped me in my tracks.

It is a most beautiful vantage point to admire the city from. I often take a second or two to gaze out across it, but this morning it arrested me and I didn't succumb to the feeling that I should be getting on with the post, choosing to linger instead.

With the sun rising from above and behind, the valley before me was cloaked in a hazy translucence, still and warm. Just across the quiet road, beyond a fence painted green, Knowle's allotment patches reached out into the valley before dropping down the steep hillside. The allotments were messy but lively, in the way that a good allotment should be, and many a bee was to be seen being industrious and dutiful, in a way that I was refusing to be in that particular moment.

Where the allotments sloped out of view, the medley of terraced housing in the distant below took its place. From here, each house looked no larger than the centimetre they were allotted in the frames in the sorting office, but the reality of the streets is that they are infinitely more chaotic than the orderly rows and columns to which they have been assigned. The streets below me lay like an assortment of matchsticks that had been tossed on a table, running higgledy-piggledy at strange angles from one another. The postal system had figured out a way to pick up these matchsticks and stack them neatly back into their box, installing a sense of order to the utter confusion that permeates the world. When one stands back and considers how the postal system has to account for all the quirks of real life, it is impossible not to respect the service it provides. No doubt a dozen posties were methodically making their way back and forth along the row of houses down there as I gazed across Bristol: a result of centuries of evolution of the postal system.

Raising my gaze again, the distant hills guarding the south edge of the city stood stoically in the morning mist. A church spire poked out of the top of these faraway deciduous forests and a flock of birds drifted above. How wonderfully green Bristol can seem, I thought to myself, if observed from the right viewpoint.

I turned with a sigh and found myself looking down the road where my next bundle of letters would lead me. It too was a picture of green. Verdurous hedges overflowed from front gardens, dogged ivy climbed up the sides of houses, and cherry blossom trees lined up on both sides of the road to cast a dappled shade on Lilymead Avenue. It was a very beautiful road, as they go, and a rather grand one too. The road and the pavements were capacious, and the front gardens large enough that some had been converted into driveways for expensive cars. In a pinch, a pilot of a small aircraft could probably have landed on Lilymead Avenue if they needed to, such was its width, although probably to the detriment of the fancy cars, not to mention the postman.

As I was reflecting, an elderly man and his elderly dog crept up on me. I suspect it had been a good few years since either of them had crept up on anything and they both looked rather pleased with themselves when they made me jump.

"Mornin' Bill!" the elderly man grinned a toothless grin. His old collie dog yawned and sat down heavily.

"Morning sir," I breathed, "you gave I a bit of a start!"

You probably wouldn't have expected me to Bristolise a sentence, but I have the unfortunate – albeit not uncommon – tendency to mirror an accent if I hear one. There's also an expectation, I think, that if I'm bringing someone in Bristol their post then it should be accompanied with a Bristol inflection, and I don't want to disappoint. Therefore, when I'm a postie, I'm a postie of Bristol. Or at least I try to be.

"I did," the old man grinned harder. "I did, didn't I?"

"That you did," I couldn't help but agree, seeing as I had said it myself.

"But you didn't ask me why I called you Bill," he pointed out.

"No, that's true I didn't, did I?"

He clearly wished that I would ask this very question, for he stood before me, mouth still smiling, eyes peering out expectantly. His dog stared at me with an uncannily similar expression.

"Alright," I said, "why did you call me Bill?"

"Because that's all you ever bring me!" The elderly man wheezed some laughter out and grinned so hard I feared for the integrity of his jaw. The collie panted a smile.

I smiled back – it was a new one to me. I started to say as much but he considered his conversational duties complete for the day and the pair were already making their way down the road. I watched them walk along against the backdrop of the Bristol vista, before pulling a satchel over my shoulder and setting off to see what lay within for Lilymead Avenue.

Bills, no doubt.

Praying small aircraft avoid your road,

P.

P.S. THE PUBS HAVE REOPENED!

LETTER TWENTY-FOUR

If there is one round that can rival the despicableness of Walk Fifty-Three, it is its neighbouring round: Walk Fifty-Two. Just on the other side of Wells Road and based in Totterdown, the postie on Walk Fifty-Two delivers to houses on the side of such a steep hill that I wouldn't be surprised if they travel more in altitude than they do in distance over the course of the day. Totterdown is reportedly home to the steepest street in the UK – Vale Street – and even if that were not true, it still tells you all you need to know about what a day of posting in Totterdown might be like.

Indeed, Vale Street is so steep that the cars have to park at an angle across it, rather than parallel with it, save they should start sliding down in the middle of the night. Standing at the bottom of Vale Street and looking up, one is taken by two things. Firstly, how quickly one's neck aches simply from trying to see the top of it. Secondly, at the bottom of it there are deep, ugly grooves in the road. These confused me to begin with, until one day I saw a car drive carefully to the bottom of Vale Street – very slowly, as one would – and as it arrived at the spot of the deep, ugly grooves in the road, a terrible screeching noise emitted from underneath it. The grooves, it turned out, are scars left by cars routinely scraping the bottom.

The history of Totterdown, however, is even more galling than its hills. If one were posting in Totterdown in the late 1960s, two things would be different. Firstly, there would be a lot more of it to post to. And secondly, you would find yourself posting a lot of eviction notices and compulsory purchase orders. When I say a lot, I mean hundreds. Indeed, in 1968, the residents were ordered to leave and what was known as 'Middle Totterdown' was swiftly obliterated.

Bristol, like so many cities in the 1960s, had been riding the wave of privatised car ownership, and the council had grown desperate to drive the city forward by building some fantastical, futuristic urban motorway. Members of the council must have really hated sitting in traffic, because what they did to try and avoid it proves they were willing to do so at all costs, whereby the costs fell squarely and heavily on the people of Totterdown. Indeed, they devised an outer circuit road around Bristol, the logistics of which demanded a sprawling spaghetti junction, a charming, curling concrete carriageway. It would sit just south of the river. Just where the traffic was giving them so much grief. Just, as the residents were soon to find out, where Middle Totterdown was.

The first that the residents heard of this was when a letter appeared telling them they were standing on the spot where one of many delightful concrete pillars were soon to be erected. They were being bought out. It was happening, happening soon, and there was nothing they could do about it.

In order to fully immerse oneself in quite how fantastically stupid and evil these sudden evictions were, it's worth dwelling on the fact that at this point Bristol council had no government approval, no funding in place, no finalised road design and had not even voted on it themselves. Presumably they thought they might as well just get on with taking down Totterdown, like it were a stack of cards, and the rest of the project would all fall neatly into place. And so 550 homes and local businesses were quickly destroyed, a thriving community of thousands of people was dispersed and lost, and one-third of Totterdown was flattened with the stroke of a pen.

At least the city benefited from a nice new road, you might be thinking. There are always losers in the pursuit of progress, after all. Alas, the ampersanding atrocity was never built. Middle Totterdown lay as a wasteland for a decade and all the problems that come with inner-city wastelands accompanied it. What had once been a bustling neighbourhood, with a cinema, pubs and a shopping hub that all Bristolians would cross the river to visit, was now derelict land host to fly-tipping and the occasional travelling community. In the 1980s, after many years of nothing happening, the council quietly accepted that their road would never be built and so some architecture befitting of the time was quickly erected. Whereas before there stood quaint Victorian terraces and businesses run by local people, there now squats some appalling concrete flats and a Tesco Express.

The feeling of betrayal tore through the Totterdown community as powerfully as the bulldozers through their homes and to this day there are still many families hurt by what happened. As former resident Elise Laurence put it, "The planners did to us what the war could not." Namely, levelled their neighbourhood and destroyed their lives.

I'm not sure I've ever found the history of town planning as affecting as in the case of Totterdown. Even writing about it now, I'm genuinely appalled by it. On the other hand, I'm relieved for Russell at least, for he's the one who has to post there. Russell, you will recall, is the postie I heard singing his Bob Marley 'Preppin'' song on my first day with Patricia and who recommends dying just after tea. Russell, who I suspected might not be fully in charge of his faculties. Well, I'm fairly confident that if Middle Totterdown still stood and he had to post to all those houses on top of all the ones he already does post to, then Russell truly would have lost his mind a long time ago. So there is that.

Three cheers to Bristol council for wiping out an entire community for the sake of Russell,

P.

LETTER TWENTY-FIVE

25th July

There are two elderly people's accommodation on Walk Fifty-Three. In one the residents are – to put it politely – a little more lively than in the other. In the late morning of each day in the livelier of the accommodations, a gang of octogenarians gathers in the communal room and invariably they have a riot of a time, relatively speaking.

Having punched the code into the door (it is unnerving how many access codes have been entrusted to me), two things are immediately apparent. One, is how unambiguously, unfathomably and unnecessarily hot the building is; and two, is the level of commotion coming from the communal room just around the corner of the hall.

When I walk through these doors I have a particularly heavy satchel because this building is on a very heavy loop. This, despite the fact that I have left several parcels in the van that I will deliver once the loop is done and I am driving back north along Wells Road. At this stage of my day I am also tiring and giving great thought to whether 10am is too early to eat my lunch.

So by the time I enter this chatty furnace, I'm not feeling all that chatty. I want to sneak past the communal room, hop in the lift to the next floor to deliver the post and be back out in the fresh air (or as fresh as the air is by a main road) where nobody bothers me save for the man with his Bill joke.

But more often than not one of the eagle-eyed elders spots me from their chair as I try to sneak by. When this happens, I am done for. I will spend what feels like an hour politely entertaining this gang of elders and their benevolent nonsense. They expect me to hand out their post one by one, as if they're the royal family awaiting missives from across the land some centuries ago. I can see that they're enjoying it all. The excitement of who has mail, who doesn't have mail and the squeal-inducing days when somebody even has a parcel that they can all watch in great anticipation as it is unwrapped. I have to stand there and observe the unwrapping too because they refuse to tell me who lives at number twenty-six until we have all seen how cosmically slowly Norman is able to unpack his latest medication pills.

Once the giddiness of that has blown over, we can get back to the letters. Even that takes a long time because these conniving pensioners enlist their delaying tactic again once there is only one letter left. If there is only one letter left, they cannily surmise, that means many of them will still be waiting for a distant cousin, or a friend from school who they haven't seen since 1953, to write back to them. As before, they won't tell me which of them the last letter belongs to, this time because they need me to witness the conversation of the displeasure of Royal Mail as a service. ("Normally they'd have written by now! The postal office must have lost it! Do you know where it is Mr Postman?")

What's palpable, however, is that beneath the thin veneer

of grumbling is a swelling pleasure in the communal activity of complaining about an institution such as Royal Mail, loved by the public almost as much for its faults as its merits. Beneath my own veneer of disgruntlement, I too am secretly enjoying this gossiping gang of grandparents before me. It's as British as it comes: post, disappointment, grumbling… what more does our public ask for? But I am helplessly aware of the outrageous temperature of their building, as well as the cold hard fact that I could have easily had the post into their letterboxes in a fraction of this time. As such I quietly pop the last letter onto the arm of a chair and slip away from the ongoing frenzy into the fresh(ish) air of Bristol.

But *there* it is, I realised today. *That's* where it's all gone wrong for the postal service. There was a time when it would have been my unwritten duty to entertain people's nonsense, because they didn't have anybody else to tell it to. Posties used to be so much more than just a bringer of mail: they brought company and relief too. They could be there to make sure someone was doing alright, to see if they needed anything or anyone, and just to spend a few minutes on the doorstep with them.

What a truly wonderful thing that is! For a lonely person to know that, for all their isolation, somebody was visiting them each day. What support that provided them, what a community that must have fostered!

But the value of this is lost in the accounting books. Kindness doesn't pay wages and it certainly doesn't turn a profit. Some years ago the government forgot that there was value in things beyond the realms of gross domestic product, and as a number couldn't be put against kindness they threw kindness out to the private companies to gobble up and do what they do best: make money out of it.

With that, the modern postie is pulled in two directions. One arm is tugged by the lingering feeling that they are part of the community and providing a service to the public, which the elderly recognise most keenly because that was what they always knew. So when a postie walks into a building in which many of these elderly folk abide, they grab this one arm and pull you in, expecting you to have the time to hang around and chat for a bit. It's not their fault that they can't see that a postie's other arm is being tugged back out the door by the invisible forces of efficiency and profit that have increased their workload so much that they simply don't have the time for this quick chat.

Time can be made, you might suggest, but you have to understand that a postie's every step is being counted. Not only every step, but also every moment there is *not* a step. Indeed, for every moment lingered in a doorway, information is being fed back from the technological devices in our pockets – the ones we ask you to sign for your parcels on – and being fed back into a system. A system that can bring up our results at the end of each day and show how fast we did our job. I have never known a manager to go up to a postie and congratulate them on how quickly they got their work done, but many a postie has known when they have not moved fast enough.

Must dash,

P.

A SHORT MISSIVE ON BEING NEEDED

Dear Elderly Sir,

It was very sweet of you to toddle quickly to your door this morning to express your gratitude towards me. You told me that I should stay safe and that you needed me. It almost brought a tear to my eye, in these emotional times. We all need each other, as it goes, though we seldom say it.

Yours eternally or until my contract is terminated (whichever comes sooner),

P.

LETTER TWENTY-SIX

4th August

"Sorry I'm in me underwear," the man at number thirty-nine apologised to me today.

It had been a warm night. Enough so that as I stepped out through my front door and into the world this morning, I found it bright and bereft of that early chill that we are so accustomed to when the summer's sky is clear. But the clouds that had covered and insulated the night were just lazing their way over to the eastern horizon, leaving a delicious blue-and-yellow sunrise over an already temperate Bristol. It was as if somebody had pulled back the snug bed sheets expecting to find it cold, but instead the heating had already come on and the house was pleasant. In fact, it was so pleasant that I cycled to work in only my Royal Mail polo shirt, rather than with a jacket over the top as I would usually. I felt as warm as the people in the hot air balloons above must have done whenever the flame came on and kept them hovering magically up there.

(Equally, I was paranoid that passers-by and hot air

balloon floaters alike would see me cycling through the city at 6am in my Royal Mail uniform and think, "Oh there goes the postie, doing the early rounds on his bike, how nice.")

So, in fairness to the man at number thirty-nine, it was sufficiently warm that one might start the day in only one's underpants. Indeed, I wouldn't have held it against the man if he had answered the door in only his underpants. The thing is, he didn't.

"Sorry I'm in me underwear," he said, fully dressed. I studied him for a moment for a trace of irony, but found none. Making the decision that it wasn't worth contradicting him, I smiled, told him not to worry, and passed him his parcel. If a man wants to be in his underwear in his own home, imaginatively or otherwise, let him be, I say.

I have had a series of interesting scenarios with people in varying states of undress, some being more desirable than others, it's fair to say.

There was, of course, the unpleasant incident of the postie in the towel that I wrote to you of in my first weeks. The spiteful man so determined to get in the shower he couldn't spare a second to answer the door. He was the polar opposite of the man at number thirty-nine, really, who had shyly but quickly answered the door in the misguided belief he was scantily clad.

Actually, I suppose the polar opposite to the man at number thirty-nine, is the man I once delivered to who was utterly, starkly, unapologetically naked.

"Oh aye, 'im," Little Larry had grinned at me when I got back to the van and told him. "Yeah, 'e ain't worn clothes since 1997."

"Why didn't you warn me?" I asked.

"Well, I don't really think abou' it no more, I suppose," he philosophised, "Don't do no 'arm, do 'e?"

"No harm," I conceded, "but he did make me come into his house and put the parcel on the kitchen table."

"Yeah, 'e does ask us that," he admitted, "but 'e ain't too sharp on 'is feet no more."

"No, that's true," I nodded. "Warning would have been nice though."

It isn't always so traumatic. Given how many doors a postie knocks on each day, it's inevitable someone will be getting in or out of their clothes for one reason or another. Once I knocked on an apartment door that was duly flung open to reveal an empty corridor. I stood puzzled for a moment, when suddenly a wet head appeared sideways from around the corner. Even at its horizontal disposition and with a string of wet hair cascading towards the floor, water dripping down freely, it was evident that the head belonged to that of a beautiful woman, who had jumped straight out the shower.

"I'm so sorry!" She exclaimed. "I'm *really* naked!"

Caught somewhere between mesmerisation and the endeavour not to be weird about this unexpected turn of events, I mumbled that it was quite alright, held out her parcel at arm's length so as to not be in anyway encroaching and quickly shuffled off. I spent the rest of the day thinking that: one, she really had no need to be so apologetic; and two, the inclusion and emphasis on the word *really* was a fascinating one and a curious spring in my step accompanied me for the rest of my round.

On days like today, however, one's spring quickly finds itself buckling under the heat. Give me a work day of rain over that of a hot summer's day every time! For if it rains I can wrap myself in layers, don my orange coat and pull up my hood. Let the letters get wet, it is no problem for me.

But on those days when the sun beats down and there is not a breath of wind in the air? There is nowhere to hide on those days. The best I have found is the large-brimmed sun hat that Royal Mail provides us with, and that does work to cool the head and neck rather well. But it is not like I have the luxury of some of these people in their houses, stripping down to nothing and waiting for the postie's knock so they can gloat at the liberty the inside of one's house provides them. No, I cannot shed so much as a sock, and am instead trapped below the beating sun with the heat radiating off pavement and walls. The city is a furnace by midday, so much so you can smell the petrochemicals seeping out of the roads, and for the ensuing three hours – the hottest of any day – I sweat my way through my shirt and through the rest of my round.

A heatwave is no time to be a postie, and if things keep on going the way they're going I shouldn't be surprised if they have to introduce a siesta to this country, so that the posties and other outside folk can take shelter from the worst of the summer sun and come back later in the day to finish the job.

Sweltering regards,

P.

P.S. It's been nice not to think about that virus too much lately, don't you think? Strange that you can't order your pints at the bar though...

LETTER TWENTY-SEVEN

13th August

Yesterday a bulldog appeared between my legs and that is not the sort of thing that a postie wants to report. How remarkable, though, that it should already be August in this year of writing to you and it is the first time that I should bring up the topic most associated with posties. Well, perhaps the third most, after a peculiar insistence on striking and that of wearing shorts.

Dogs! Man's greatest friend, the loyal mammal we invite into our homes to feed, care for and love like a child. In return we ask for little more than that they keep an eye on things for us: have a good sniff around the garden, have a good woof at anybody that walks up to the house and have a good go at trying to acquire the fingers of a postie.

There were precisely 2,445 dog attacks on posties across the country last year. Quite what warrants an 'attack' I'm not sure, but in any case it's a large number. It's nearly seven dog attacks each day, meaning on average that about once an hour during shift-time a dog is having a nibble on a postie somewhere across the country.

There are various ways Royal Mail tries to mitigate these dog attacks and they vary wildly in effectiveness. The most effective is the rule that if a dog is in the front garden of a property, we don't go in. That's a pretty watertight strategy for returning home with all the bodily bits that you took to work that morning. The least effective, to my mind, is the plastic posting peg we are bestowed with on our first day of work. It looks a bit like a ruler out of a child's pencil case, although it is coloured red, has no measurements on it, and is tightly tonged such that it can just about hold onto a letter. We are supposed to carry this with us at all times and post letters through the door with them, so that when we with-draw our hand we don't find any of our digits missing in action. It might sound like a sensible idea, but in reality this plastic posting peg is about as practical as the proverbial chocolate teapot and I've never met a postie who even carries theirs, let alone uses it.

I guess I was one of the lucky ones to begin with. For a long time I never had a dog appear out of nowhere and startle me, and I was beginning to wonder how any postie had even lost a fing–

WHOOSH! Just like that, the teeth of a dog grazed the very end of my fingertips. I jumped back from the letterbox and toppled back down the steps behind me. The dog launched into a barking bonanza on the other side of the door, presumably devastated he hadn't secured at least a fingernail. Up until that moment I had always been vigilant not to let my fingers go all the way through a letterbox if I heard barking inside, but this particular canine had gone into stealth mode at the sound of my approach. The moment a layer of skin was poking through his letterbox, he lunged. He missed by mere millimetres.

I became much more diligent after that, and was sure never to put so much as a pinkie all the way through a letterbox. Sooner or later, though, all posties find themselves face to face with a dog. Or, as in my case yesterday, they find one between their legs.

I had rushed to the front door of the 479th house for the day (or something thereabouts) on a walk I had never done before, when a noise from below alerted me to the bulldog's presence. Stunned, and more than a little disconcerted, I could only surmise that he had charged through the door itself to emerge there. But as I quickly withdrew from the letterbox I had been reaching for, I realised there was a camouflaged dog flap in the door that I had not seen. I had never seen a dog flap in any door before, in fact, and for a moment I started pondering on when dog flaps became a thing. Then the bulldog found its bearings, rounded on me, and I had other concerns.

The situation became chillingly clear, as it might have done years ago on some faraway savannah. A wolf with a set of teeth versus a human with a weapon. Unfortunately, the passing of time has meant that while the wolf has kept its teeth, my modern-day weapon was an A5 paper envelope.

Though nobody had taught us to, both the bulldog and I each assumed an attacking stance of sorts, albeit mine looking a lot more shaky. I told myself to remain calm. As it happens, one bark of warning from the bulldog saw me lose said calm and with a quick yelp I aimed my only weapon at it. The bulldog watched the letter sail harmlessly over its large head, settling somewhere in the far corner of the garden, thereby leaving me defenceless. Defenceless, that is, save for the satchel on my back, which I now pulled around to my front such that it could be a shield. Just like those Royal Mail training videos had taught me all those months ago. My satchel, however, was empty and I wasn't feeling particularly protected by any stretch of the imagination.

The bulldog sensed this was its moment to strike. It bowed its great head, leaned back on its legs and prepared to charge. Unhelpful visions of my body lying strewn across the front garden came to mind, a British bulldog with a bobbing head sitting alongside, triumphant and smug, saying "Oh yes!" on repeat.

At that moment a roar emitted from an upstairs window, transforming my adversary from a wild beast to a whimpering baby. It was such a noise that it nearly exploded my own thumping heart, but clearly the danger was over. As the bulldog scampered back through its flap like a snail into its shell, I looked up and saw the owner had poked her head out of the upstairs window.

"Sorry 'bout Terence," she said sweetly, as though she hadn't just screamed the local animal kingdom back into their lairs.

"Yep," was just about all I could manage, and I walked away quite shaken.

I had never seen a dog flap before the day a bulldog shot out of one and as fate would have it I would fail to see another one this morning too. Again, I was rushing around a walk I had never done before and again a dog came rushing out between my legs at the sound of the letterbox. I couldn't believe it. I'd gone from never seeing a dog flap before in my life to seeing two in two days, and here was another dog rounding on me.

Well, fortunately the owner of this one was much more prompt in his response. He came casually out of the door (not via the dog flap, but the human flap), swooped down to pick up the snarling little canine, and started chatting merrily away about how he didn't recognise me and I must not have known about the dog. I didn't have the energy to explain quite how startling it was to have this happen on a daily basis, so nodded meekly and retreated into the world once again.

What Royal Mail don't seem to have given a lot of consideration to is not putting their staff under obscene levels of pressure to post more parcels and letters every year. Or to providing the sorting office managers with sufficient resources such that they aren't forced to put new posties on a new walk for every new day of the week. These are the things that would genuinely help to prevent dog attacks, because it's when posties are under pressure or when they're unfamiliar with an area that mistakes are much more likely to be made. Indeed, if Royal Mail chose not to systematically understaff their company – and it is something that they have chosen to do – they would find that their employees have a more realistic workload. Then posties would be far less likely to rush into front gardens without checking for dogs, or hastily stuff their hand into a letterbox, only to get back to the warehouse and realise they lost an index finger somewhere between Jersey Avenue and Birchwood Road.

But what do I know? I'm just a postie.

Your just-a-postie,

P.

LETTER TWENTY-EIGHT

21st August

"Mornin' Bill!" cried the elderly man with the old sheepdog.

"Mornin'," I dutifully replied.

"You know why's I call you Bill, don't you?" Man and dog both looked at me, expectantly.

"Because that's all I bring you?"

"That's right," man and dog smiled as one. Then he said, "My uncle was a postie, you know."

"Is that so?"

"He ain't no more, mind," the elderly man sighed. "Up in the 'ead office now." He looked to the sky. So did the dog. So did I.

Rain was falling lightly on the hot concrete of the city, pushing up both humidity and sweet-smelling petrichor from the pavements. I suggested to the elderly man his uncle was probably having a chuckle at us, out here in this rainy British summer. He looked up again as if noting the rain for the first time.

"Oh, well," the elderly man shrugged. The dog tilted its head.

"You both best get home before it pours," I said politely, keen to get on with my round.

"We will, Bill," he winked, "I can see yer busy."

Then he looked me up and down, studied my beshorted legs for a moment, and said, "Try and look after yerself."

Then he and the dog turned and moved slowly home. I watched him go, a gentle, shepherd-like figure, and felt the familiar pang of guilt that I didn't chat longer. No doubt he was lonely, save for his loyal dog, and hankered for a time when the postie did stop to talk. He might as well have been a shepherd out in the rolling hills: you'd get more chat from a sheep than from me.

Interactions like this make me question what it means to be a postie. I could have spoken to the Shepherd, as I think of him now, for another few minutes today. Certainly by the standards of the past, this would make me a good postie: being sociable and keeping an eye out for the people. But what if a few minutes of chat becomes the expectation for every day, and what if I then pick up some other strays on the street and all of a sudden I'm clocking thirty or forty minutes of chatting every shift? My managers are going to notice that. They'll look into the data on my device and see that I'm pausing for ten minutes here and there, and they'll ask questions. They could even come out and watch me to see what's going on. It happens.

In this day and age then, should a good postie rush around, delivering to as many houses and taking out as many extra parcels as their van can carry? Well, this approach is fraught with problems too. Working heroic shifts to clear the letters from a walk that hasn't been taken out for days, or piling the parcels of several Yorks into your van, are not seen as heroic shifts by the managers. Rather, they just prove what they have suspected all along: that posties could work harder. In achieving the impossible, one is only raising the bar of the acceptable.

The figure of the Shepherd was turning into a distant dot and the drizzle into a determined downpour. But I stayed put.

I'll admit, at first I suspected the same as the managers: that the long-serving posties did the bare minimum and were never willing to put their shoulder to the wheel to ease the workload on anyone else. But after some nine months of throwing my shoulder against that wheel, I can see why the experienced posties no longer bother. Because in taking on more and more work, you are only thwarting your colleagues. If I worked my little cotton socks off trying to clear a walk – thinking that it would benefit the colleague who then didn't have to do it – all it would really mean was that the managers expected more from their staff. The more successful our managers were at squeezing this labour out of us, the more *their* managers wanted to squeeze labour from them, and so on and so on, right the way to the top. So I would find that my workload only ever piled higher, but when work only begets more work, there's no incentive to work at all.

With these dreary thoughts I turned away from the speck of the Shepherd and walked through the rain in the opposite direction. Arthur had warned me of thundery showers from his usual spot this morning and here it was. I was soaked through.

The old timers have had this all figured out for decades and now I could see precisely where they were coming from. And so the modern-day postie finds themselves in a catch twenty-two: if we don't work harder, we do wrong by those we serve; if we do work harder, we do wrong by those with whom we serve. The only winners are those at the top who continue to get richer for doing less, while the posties work harder, for longer, for less, and the lonely public get lonelier still.

I walked on. I walked through puddles warmed by the heat of the pavement and felt hot water seeping through to my feet. I walked until the re-emerged sun cleared the clouds from the sky and sucked the rain from the roads. I walked until all the post and parcels were delivered and I could go home to come back again tomorrow.

Thy humble bringer of bills,

P.

LETTER TWENTY-NINE

11th September

It was the most peculiar of mornings, and it is not often that a postie gets to say that. A postie's morning is so orderly and precise that time itself could set its watch by our movements. Posties, as you know, can do their job without so much as opening their mouths (though only a select few have the capacity to shut them), and they could also probably arrive to work still in their sleep and get on with their work seamlessly, such is the routine and predictability of it. We are, without doubt, a product of the Industrial Revolution that so readily blurred the line between man and machine. Indeed, the postie is to Royal Mail as the cog is to the machine, and from the moment we wake up we are set to turn precisely as the machinery has instructed us.

But not this morning. My programme started as per usual: legs swinging out of bed before the alarm even began to ring; cycling among the seagulls at the harbour in the cool morning air; bracing myself for what I would find on the other side of the swinging doors through to the warehouse...

All manner of things have awaited me on the other side of those swinging doors: a choir of posties singing about socks, a mayhem of managers running about with buckets to catch rain from the leaking roof, a whole warehouse of posties that had spontaneously decided to balance a parcel of their choosing on their heads for the morning... Once I think I even saw a manager smile beyond those swinging doors, though it might have been a trick of the light.

What I have never seen before though, is *nothing*. No post. No parcels. No posties. Nothing but empty frames, silent walls and no fluorescent lights.

My first thought was that I'd come in on a Sunday accidentally. But even on a Sunday posties work these days. There are many that need the overtime and the managers are always desperate to keep on top of the impossible workloads. So even on a Sunday there wouldn't be *nothing*.

Gary appeared from the manager's office and found me standing there, puzzled by the peace and quiet. He grinned at me. Maybe it is Sunday, I thought to myself, Gary probably wouldn't know either way.

"Alright?" He said.

"What's this?" I demanded.

"Bomb scare, innit," he replied, nonchalantly.

"A bomb?" I blurted, "in here?"

"Nah," he smiled, "not in 'ere'"

"Well, where?"

"Dunno," Gary shrugged, "ain't 'ere though."

A manager came out of his office with a little more information to offer than Gary was able to. Royal Mail, he explained, had received a call about a "dangerous package", and the threat had been deemed to be viable. The caller had provided a tracking code that matched an item currently in the system and so the police were taking it seriously. The package in question was either in Bristol or in Bath, but the tracking system couldn't be more accurate than that, which just about sums up Royal Mail's tracking system.

Royal Mail had stopped all post in the Bristol and Bath area for the day. We were free to go home, the manager explained. He said it in a way such that he was doing me a great service, rather than keeping me from posting a bomb to somebody in the next few hours.

And so that's just what I did. Go home, I mean, not post a bomb. The only thing more delightful than a day off work is an unexpected day off work. It's like the snow day that hadn't been forecast but has shut the schools. The problem, of course, is that the teachers then have to catch you up with the lessons that you have missed, and in much the same way we will have to work twice as hard to post two days of work tomorrow. If the sorting office hasn't been blown up, that is.

I cycled home the long way and found the city bathed in splendour. The morning sun blazed down on Bristol and the sky was an untainted denim blue, save for the lingering full moon that hung just above the horizon, white and tender. Rays of sunlight exploded off the River Avon, which at high tide seems imperishably brown but at low tide this morning I found sparkling emerald green and lively with bathing gulls. Great oak trees lined the banks and squirrels busied themselves in corkscrew fashion up and down their trunks. I paused in the shade of one of these ancient trees to admire the church of St Phillips, jutting quaintly out of Bedminster's greenery across the rushing water, and – fooled by my stillness – a determined squirrel scurried close by. (It is indeed a scurry of squirrels, in case you were wondering.) The squirrel clenched a bright green acorn between its teeth, freshly plucked and prime for burying ahead of darker days. I took it as a sure sign of a fading summer.

But the day was young, the real heat was still to come and it was entirely my own. I sit and pen this to you at my desk looking out over the city – as the evening oozes a sweet, earthly smell – and feel serene and grateful. Who knew a bomb could be so calming?

With unabashed smugness,

P.

A SHORT MISSIVE ON
DANGEROUS PACKAGES

Dear Gary,

They found the bomb. It was in the Bath sorting centre. They blew the bugger up. Turns out it was a hoax all along.

Phew,

P.

LETTER THIRTY

17th September

Today I stepped on a snail.

I make a point of not stepping on snails. I keep an eye out for them in between glancing at the addresses on the letters and I move them out of harm's way if I think they could use the help. I mean, I know I'd be unhappy if anybody stepped on me.

Sometimes, it cannot be otherwise. When you're walking along looking at the next letter, or when you turn down a garden path and you've got your eyes set on the letterbox, ready to whip that letter into it as quickly as drawing a pistol from a hip, you aren't necessarily watching the ground. Occasionally, as you turn on your heel, heroically leaving yet another letterbox reeling in your wake, you hear a fatal *crunch* from below. You immediately know what you have done, and you know that if you were to lift your foot up and check, the shell of the once-snail would be spread like a mosaic across the concrete. So I don't check in those cases, and I don't feel remorse, because though it is sad, it is life. Such are the casualties of posting.

But this is not what happened today. Today, I murdered a snail and as I write this I feel terrible remorse.

Had I spotted the creature on another day – a better day, when I had been a better version of myself – I would have crouched down to them, plucked them gently off the ground, and placed them softly and safely in the direction of their steady travel. There have been days where I have helped a dozen such snails, heedlessly ploughing out across land prone to footfall and car wheels, but I shall have to save many dozens, perhaps hundreds more, before I atone for today's act. Or perhaps it doesn't matter how many more I save now. Perhaps there is no atonement.

My excuse, feeble as it sounds now, is that I was having among the worst days of work I have ever known. When it rains on a postie it pours and today was torrential.

I arrived this morning in the belief that I would be on Walk Fifty-Three, which I have worked so hard to stay on top of this week. The amount coming through the system is skyrocketing at the moment: the number of parcels is completely unprecedented, even by Christmas standards. The number of staff off sick is rising at a similar rate and I haven't heard singing in the sorting office for many weeks now.

But this morning I was assigned to Walk Fifty-Two in Totterdown. That one I was telling you about with the steep hill and the demolished history. The one that I said was the worst walk in our postcode area.

There's nothing wrong with Totterdown, incidentally, other than the fact that it was built on the side of a steep hill. It is so steep that if ice settles overnight in Totterdown, when the residents step out of their front doors in the morning they immediately slide to the bottom, where they collect in one big fleshy heap. The Totterdownians are used to this though, so they stand up, brush the ice off their neighbours and go about their day.

It may not have been icy, but the Totterdown walk to which I was assigned had not been dealt with all week. The boxes of letters and bags of parcels – which for this walk were formidable even on a normal day – now formed an impenetrable fortress around the frame.

"Just take what you can," the manager said, as he observed me observing the fortress. He scuttled off before I could argue that it's all very well and good to say "take what you can", but there was simply so much of it that it would take me half a day just to put even a fraction of it into something vaguely resembling orderliness. I could hardly just bung it all in the van, drive manically to Totterdown and hope it had magically arranged itself into order on the way there.

I waded into those bags and boxes at 6.30am, and it wasn't until 11am that I had managed to put it into some sort of arrangement such that I could actually post it in a half-efficient way. I was already seething.

It took another half an hour to load the van until it was so full I had to take a running jump at the back door so that it would close properly. Having climbed into the driver's seat and turned the engine on, the fuel gauge immediately flashed red and beeped at me. That was the first roar of frustration that I let out at the steering wheel. (Posties play a game of chicken with the fuel in the van. It's in nobody's interest to go and top it up as it takes precious time out of one's day, so nobody does it until the gauge is so far down it would be beyond foolish to risk it. Today, of all days, it was that far down.)

I got back out the van and went into the office to sign out the credit card to go and buy fuel. I was supposed to return the card immediately, but it was approaching midday and I had a full van and an extremely long day ahead still. So I drove straight out to Totterdown and, as the clock hit noon, I finally put a letter through a door.

I wrote to you previously that if your day has started off badly, there is no hope for you: it will only get worse. This is a very reliable rule in the life of a postie. The morning had riled me and I was now a walking, ticking time bomb. Everything made me more agitated: the wind that licked at the flimsy advertising I was trying to direct into a letterbox; the garden gate that jarred on the ground as I hurriedly pushed against it; the houses of Totterdown all higgledy-piggledy on the hill, running in no systematic order whatsoever.

It was raining, of course. On a better day I might have referred to it whimsically as a summer shower. But no, today it was simply rain: heavy, cold, unwanted. I was an elastic band being stretched, soon to snap.

I returned to my van after a couple of hours to find that I had scarcely made a dent in the workload, and things more or less spiralled irretrievably downwards from there. At first I mindlessly put the van key down somewhere to reach to the back corner of the van and prise a parcel out so that I could deliver to a house across the road. Never – if you are so foolish as to become a postie – put your key down in the back of a loaded van. Dark and congested as it was back there, I spent the ensuing ten minutes rifling around looking for where I had put it. The rifling began carefully enough, but by the fourth minute it was manic and pitiful.

I found the key after the tenth minute – it had been in my coat pocket all along – and so I walked over the road with this parcel that had caused me so much stress. I thrust it into the person's startled hands – very rudely so – and turned on my heel to march back to the van. The person then called me over, which always agitates me because I am clearly very important and in a hurry, and I don't need their unnecessary nonsense in my day. As it was, I had given this person the wrong parcel, perhaps unsurprisingly given the above, and so I sheepishly returned a minute later with the correct one.

And so continued my day. The rain fell harder, the sky got darker and eventually I snapped like the proverbial elastic band. It was catching my hand on a nail in a letterbox that did it. Sounds dangerous, doesn't it? Well it blooming well is and yet it's not the first nail in a letterbox my hands have been sliced on, nor will it be the last.

I stomped off down the pavement and that's when I did it. I'd like to say I don't know what came over me, but I can still taste the pure anger that I felt as I directed my foot down on the snail crossing my path. I know that it was unmistakably human anger and that it can make humans do unforgivable things. I felt wronged and I was lashing out at the world by doing evil to a snail so that I could even the scales. I felt no better for it, of course, and now I feel only a great unhappiness about it all.

Ashamedly,

P.

P.S. I guess you saw the new rule that we've got to limit social gatherings to six? The 'Rule of Six' they're calling it. I guess if you work in the upper echelons of society that translates to the 'Rule of sixty-mile drives if you need to check if your eyes are working'.

❧ IV ❧
AUTUMN

Beauty surrounds us, but usually we need to be walking in a garden to know it.

Rumi

LETTER THIRTY-ONE

21st September

The tilt of the Earth is working against us once more and with each passing dawn there is another handful of rays missing from the sky. As the sun arrives a little later and a little more southerly, the water of the harbour is left that little bit blacker and the morning shadows stretch out that little bit further and little bit dimmer. But the air is fresher for it and I breathe in a great cold lungful before I enter the sorting office in the dim light of autumn's dawn. When I re-emerge in two or three hours' time, it will be warm, bright and hard to distinguish from a summer's day.

Within the walls of the sorting office, the tilt of the Earth is not so easily measured. The atmosphere is unchanging over the course of the year and indeed there are more constants than variables: the windowless walls, the rows of frames, the glaring lights. Even the posties seldom change. No, the only thing that might indicate the time of year is the volume of parcels or the songs on the radio. Otherwise all was enduring, and this can be no better demonstrated than in the irrepressibility of the posties when they came together in the early hours with the radio on. They were already in full flow as I flung open the doors this morning…

"Why do you build oi up (build oi up!)
Buttercup, baby!"

… the office was essentially a well-lit karaoke parlour…

"Just to let oi down (let oi down!)
And mess oi around!"

… I scribbled on the signing-in sheet and made for my frame…

"And then, worst of all (worst of all!)
Ye never call, baby
When ye say ye will (say ye will)"

… I weaved through a throng of dancing posties…

"But I love you still
I need you (I need you!)

… I ducked under a few outstretched arms…

"More than anyone, darlin'
You know that I have from the start"

… and I just about made it to the relative safety of my frame before…

"So build oi up (build oi up!)
Buttercup, don't break my 'eart…"

With the change of the season has come another change in my round. Having spent the summer mornings climbing the hills of Knowle as the mercury climbs the thermometer, now autumn has arrived I am once more to be dispersed around southeast Bristol as the heat is dispersed around the atmosphere. That is to say, I will be used as and when to cover wherever is needed across the office, covering Brislington one day, say, and Stockwood the next. It is a disadvantage not to be on one's own round that one can take care of properly day by day, but equally there is not a walk in the office I have not done now and so it is not a disaster. I think I know where all the worst dogs are, at least. Fingers crossed (and tucked).

I was posted, so to speak, to Stockwood today, and I met the most delightful lady called Anne. She was tending to her front garden and saw me coming down the road, and by the time I arrived to her she was full of topics to talk about. Was I her new postman? What did I make of it all? Was it me who cut my hand on her letterbox the other day? She was worried about spots of blood on her letters.

It wasn't me and it most likely wasn't her letterbox that caused the cut, I consoled her, but she looked at me with teary eyes as though I had lost a hand and it were all her fault. I reassured her it was quite normal to have a cut on one's hand – if you weren't bleeding Royal Mail red you were doing it all wrong, I joked – and that perked her up and we moved on to topics of the garden. It was in a splendid state, I complimented her, and she replied that she had a lot of time, and the summer had been kind.

As I look out over the city as dusk settles, the last hot air balloons of the season are touching down in far-flung fields of green, as though they are summer themselves coming into land. Gazing across to those distant fields as I write this letter to you, I reflect that it really has been a kind summer. When I was a schoolchild the long summer holidays seemed to pass by in an obstinate muggy grey, but recently they've become sharply hot and piercingly blue. It remains very hot for September – I walked into many a spider's web again today – but it is also unmistakably autumnal: this strangely comforting season where we head fearlessly into the abyss of winter.

As I left the office this morning, Earth, Wind and Fire rang out on the radio, marking the halfway point between the summer and winter solstice: the moment between the lightest and the darkest day of the year. The posties didn't hold back:

"Do yer remember?
The 21st noight of September?
Love be changin' the moinds of pretenders
While chasin' they clouds awayyy!"

The evening sky is clear, the clouds are as chased away as the hot air balloons and I am ready for autumn.

With changing seasons,

P.

LETTER THIRTY-TWO

4th October

In the mornings when I am putting the parcels into my satchels, occasionally I will find somebody has ordered something that fits nicely into a long tube and this pleases me greatly. I don't know what is in one long tube to the next, of course, but frankly I don't much care. For in my mind that long tube will be my sword, or perhaps a lightsaber, when I am out on my rounds and I will derive much pleasure from delivering it. Over the course of the day, as I return from each loop back to my van to collect the next satchel and wander off in the direction that the letters demand of me, I will be counting down to the satchel with the sword. When that loop finally arrives, and I am striding along with a bag full of bills and bog-standard parcels, I am buoyant in the knowledge that I am also secretly armed with a weapon protruding from my pouch.

As I approach the house that is taking delivery of this long-tube-come-weapon, my fingers tingle with anticipation. I take two steps up the garden path and then in one smooth motion I reach behind my back, seize the grip of the saber and wield it before me like some postman-come-Jedi going into battle. I feel powerful with the weight of it in my hand as I reach my adversary…

Knock, knock, knock…

"Yes?"

"Delivery for you."

"Ah, me poster. Cheers, then."

"Righto."

Not a sword or a lightsaber, after all. But some days this is about as exciting as it gets.

Knocking on doors is a surprisingly fraught part of my day. There is an art to it, a knack to the knock if you will, which takes some learning. If you knock too quietly you'll never get the person's attention. If you knock too loudly you'll find you get a bit too much of their attention. And if you knock when there is a bell to be rung that you did not see, then god help you.

People can be oddly delicate about the manner in which their attention is captured. I say odd because most people spend most of their days entirely unaware of just what is holding their attention, or of what is moving it from one thing to the next in any given moment. Unfortunately, a knock at the door that lands on the wrong side of one's decibel threshold seems to be a really irksome thing for people; I have many a time been berated for a knock that is too loud. As I stand there politely receiving these reprobations, I find myself wondering how they are expecting me – a never before guest of their home – to be familiar with the acoustics of the inside of their house. Not to mention the acoustics on the inside of their deranged heads.

Anyway, it's getting pretty cold here and the days are shortening. It's not long until the clocks go back, we all get plunged into a seemingly endless darkness and Gary turns up to work at the wrong time again, although at least this time he's an hour early. But the leaves are rustling sumptuously and sometimes the smell of a wood fire hangs over the streets, such that I cannot help but feel secretly glad the hedonism of summer is behind us. When a new season knocks on the door like this, the louder the better I say.

May your postie find great lark in delivering long tubes,

P.

P.S. Sounding a bit gloomy on the Covid front again isn't it? Cases on the up, folks working from home and they're closing the pubs strictly at 10pm! But I've had a word with the virus and it says it doesn't normally come out until after 10pm, so I can see where the government are coming from...

LETTER THIRTY-THREE

20th October

A little over 200 years ago on October's twentieth night, the strangest events unfolded among the darkness of Salisbury Plain. The consequences of the incident in question involved the deaths of several animals, the severe traumatisation of an individual, and – because it's how Britain likes to remember things – the creation of a long-standing pub and many a Christmas card.

It is a great – but not good – coincidence that a similar incident occurred this very week. Granted, there were no deaths and no Christmas cards shall result from it, but I was at least a little bit traumatised, and the pub nearby certainly benefited.

I'll begin with the story of the Exeter mail coach. In 1816 a mail coach was rumbling through the night from Exeter to London, when a guard saw through the dark what he believed to be a large calf. It was only later on, when one of the coach's horses was viciously attacked outside the Winterslow Hut, that he realised it was something quite different. In fairness to him, one does not expect to find a lioness on the loose on Salisbury Plain.

But a lioness on the loose it was no less, and it had celebrated its newfound freedom by mauling the lead horse of the mail coach as it stopped to deliver post to the Winterslow Hut (now known as the Phoenix Inn). Quite reasonably, all the passengers of the coach promptly alighted to run to safety, apart from one who found themselves paralysed by fear and unable to flee. History tells us they were so traumatised by the incident that they spent the rest of their days in an asylum.

How, you might be wondering, did a lioness come to be prowling the plains of Salisbury? Well, much like the animal that attacked me on my rounds yesterday: it escaped. But while the animal that I found myself confronted with had escaped the front door of its house, the lioness had escaped a travelling menagerie. Both quite careless moments on the part of the owners, if you ask me, although admittedly with quite different outcomes.

While the lioness went on to savage a large dog that had ill-advisedly joined the fray, the animal that presented itself before me was somewhat smaller in stature. I don't care what you say, though, terrier or not, those little dogs are vicious.

I knew it was bad news as soon as the young girl opened the door. The terrier was going ballistic behind her, and I could see in her eyes that she didn't have the determination to keep the dog *in* that the dog had to get *out*. I shouldn't have tried to slip the parcel through the door to her, but I panicked and wanted to be away from there immediately. I have, as it goes, been around dogs all my life, but they're a different proposition when one is a postie and now I am deeply distrustful of the conniving bastards.

He got out of the door, of course. He came yapping and scampering towards me as I hastened backwards down the driveway. It was a hairless, unloved creature and – having been stripped of its inbred purpose of chasing animals down burrows – it now came after posties that arrived to its door. You'll recall I brought an envelope to a fight with a bulldog and so I think you'll agree my chances were improved this time, in that I had a small parcel to fight off a terrier.

In the split seconds before it lunged, something inside of me decided to keep hold of my weapon this time. The small parcel was now a flimsy shield and holding it out at distance I prayed I could block the attack. But the terrier was quick, low and at full advantage. My parrying attempt missed and he soared towards my defenceless legs. Sharp teeth sunk into flesh – I was wearing shorts, of course – and I let out a cry of pain as terrier teeth tore skin. The dog swiftly retreated, content its job was done, and padded happily back through the door where the young girl stood wide-eyed and panicked. As it had retreated I turned my shield into a missile and tossed it at the dog in rage. To my distinct displeasure, I missed. Again.

I limped back down the driveway: leg bleeding, heart racing and mind fogged. It really is a horrible thing to be attacked by a dog, even one as small as a terrier. I dread to think what it must be like to be confronted by a lioness on the dark plains of Salisbury. As it happens, that attacker got away scot free too, as the menagerie keeper arrived just in time to prevent her being shot. I suspect they then all went to the pub, which is precisely what I did too.

Anyway, if you get any Christmas cards with lionesses on this year, or if you hear I'm spending some time on a psychiatric ward, you'll know why.

Drunkenly,

P.

LETTER THIRTY-FOUR

1st November

As the last letter of the day slips from the ends of my aching fingers, and arcs silently and unseen into the inside of a house, my satisfaction is quietly tremendous. It invariably feels like a very long time since I arrived at the sorting office and arranged a mass of letters – some back to front, many upside down and all out of order – into something logical and coherent, which I could then take to the streets and dispatch at what initially felt like a great speed, until my legs tired and my hands hurt and the last few streets seemed to take an age. But here I am now, with empty hands and an empty van, and all I have to do is drive back to the sorting office and cycle home.

This initial burst of happiness that comes with victory over the day tends to be short lived. In the van, with the heaters blasting and the radio on, I am exhausted and want only to be home immediately. If I am lucky, I will beat the rush-hour traffic and if I am really lucky I might beat the school run. It will be a swift roll down the hill to the industrial estate astride the river, where the southeast Bristol sorting office is nestled.

As I drove down the hill today I was not so fortunate and found myself in traffic that backed up Wells Road many a mile. It is, after all, a Friday: Bristol traffic at its very worst. I found myself gazing at the city's skyline, a confusing medley of green hills, towering architecture and a famous suspension bridge. Scaffolding wrapped itself around some of the buildings and cranes scarred the skyline. Many of them had been there for several months. It was all an ugly reminder of a beautiful truth: that everything was in a state of flux, constantly changing, updating and renewing. Just like the post, the city was never finished. There was always more to be done tomorrow.

It's one of the worst things about being a postie. The knowledge that even after the hardest of shifts, you've got to do it all again the next day. It doesn't really matter how well you did your job today, because tomorrow it will be the same. (Although as I have pointed out, there is actually a risk that the better you do your job today, the *worse* your day will be tomorrow, because your manager is likely to take advantage of your efficiency and determination.) Indeed, one feels a little like a mole that has worked all night to dig itself out of the ground, only to return the following evening to discover the hole has been filled in and all the work must start anew. (I just looked up the collective noun for moles and it's a labour. A labour of moles. A labour of posties? It's not bad. What do you think?)

On the other hand, one of the best things about being a postie is that, unlike many occupations, you don't take work home with you. In fact, they explicitly tell you not to, which is fair enough, because that would be stealing. Incidentally, an Italian postman made the news a few years ago for taking his work home with him. The problem was, of course, he never brought it back again. The post sat in his garage, hoarded for years and years, until someone started to notice that the common denominator in a lot of missing letters, was him. He went to prison, of course, where presumably he was not permitted to work in the mailroom.

Had this Italian postman worked in Britain in the 1800s, his fate would have been a whole lot worse. We really had a taste for hanging people in those days, as John Barrett discovered in 1832. Barrett was, to his great misfortune, the last postman to be hanged in Britain, committing his crime on the wrong side of the historical boundary where hanging rather went out of fashion. A London sorter, he was found guilty of stealing money from the letters that he organised. When his day came in the Old Bailey, several cases of post-pinching were brought against him. He pleaded guilty to most, but interestingly not all. Nonetheless, the fact that he had pleaded guilty to some did not let him off the hook, so to speak.

These Old Bailey cases make for fascinating reading. Shortly after Barrett learned his destiny that day, a twenty-seven-year-old man called William Glassborow stood trial for theft as well, albeit not post related. He too was sentenced to death by hanging for the crime of stealing twenty-three silver forks and twenty-one silver spoons from his master. After him stood Edward Faning, accused of stealing two coats, two shawls and a waistcoat, who was also swiftly sent to the gallows; before Henry Wells and William Freeman were then summarily found guilty of stealing two cows. One cow for each of them was presumably the idea, but if you get sent to death for stealing forks and spoons then you most certainly get sent to death for stealing a pair of heifers, and so off they went as well. We really did do a lot of hanging back then.

But it was a George Lancaster who was without doubt

most harshly done by that day. Like seemingly everyone who appeared in the Old Bailey on 5th January 1832, he too was sentenced to death. His crime? Stealing *writing paper*. His age? George was fourteen years old.

I let the handbrake off as the traffic rolled forward a few metres, before it all came to a stop again. I sighed. Traffic is the worst.

May the thousandth paper cut not slay thy postie,

P.

P.S. How was your Halloween yesterday? I thought the scariest thing to happen was the announcement of another lockdown. Bringing it into force on 5th November sounds like a recipe for disaster too... A national lockdown imposed by a government on the night of the closest thing Britain has to a celebration of anarchism? The irony could be explosive.

LETTER THIRTY-FIVE

11th November

The morning light found Bristol belatedly and briskly. The fog of last night was still yet to be dispersed and so it clung to the city at arm's length: not quite touching it, but never too far away. The shape of the sun could just about be made out low over the southeastern horizon, but it had its work cut out to dispatch the cool morning air.

I had a fair amount of dispatching to do myself and as my second winter at Royal Mail approaches I feel not that dissimilar to the sun at this time of year: we both stoop a little lower, have to work a little harder and just don't seem to shine quite as brightly.

For all of the negatives of an impending winter, on days like today one can hardly complain. Lest we forget, times were once much worse. I have to say I find the anniversary of Armistice Day to be a very affecting one. Not because I am particularly patriotic and not because I see anything glorious in war, but simply because I am a great believer in remembering how much worse one's situation could so easily be. If

I'd wanted to write these letters in George Lancaster's day, for example, I'd most likely have been strung up alongside him, the fork lifters and the cow burglars.

I have had some bad days on this job – days where the rain has been coming down as hard as it ever has – but it has never rained bullets. Perhaps it sounds ludicrous to make such a stark comparison, but personally I find it a genuinely useful perspective. It is, after all, nothing but sheer good luck that I was not born in a time of world war, and was not born in one of the many parts of the world that are currently stricken by a violent conflict of some sort. I am a postman in a safe country where I occasionally have bad days. I find the utmost comfort in that and that is why I believe in remembering Armistice Day.

There were posties even in the midst of world wars, though, did you know? And I don't just mean posties in England delivering letters between grieving countries, but posties who delivered to the beaches of Normandy in 1944. A beach is hardly an orderly place at the best of times: for starters, there is a severe lack of postcodes, the thought of which would give Little Larry postcode-traumatic stress disorder in and of itself. Nonetheless, somehow a postal system was worked out such that not only did letters reach the front, but they mostly reached the right men too. As if this weren't remarkable enough, on average it took a mere two and a half days for a letter to reach its addressee. Sixty hours! From a letter being written from the relative safety of an English house, to reaching the bloodied hands of a soldier, can you believe? It makes peacetime delivery times look decidedly sluggish.

Letters made it to the trenches in the First World War as well, and it's hard to overstate how important for morale they must have been. Keeping a soldier in touch with family – when his life was otherwise mud, rats, wet socks and worse

– was keeping a soldier in touch with what he was fighting for. There is a well-known story of a soldier writing to a newspaper expressing his loneliness and hankering for some mail, the poor chap. But after his letter was published, that same lonely soldier was the receiver of some three-thousand letters, ninety-eight large parcels and three more bags of smaller packages. If that doesn't warm your cold heart, it at least shows the value that other people attach to the postal system. It also gets one wondering where on earth he would have stored all that stuff?

But there was a lot of *stuff* going out to France in those war years: in 1916 nearly five million parcels were delivered in the month before Christmas and by 1918 there were twelve million letters being sent out *every week* from England. Royal Mail was also responsible for the things coming back: namely, the belongings of the deceased.

It's worth remembering that Royal Mail's wartime efforts were up there with heroic, though they have never really been recognised for the role they played. Perhaps that is only right given so many others gave so much more, but nonetheless the posties played their part. It is very noticeable to me when out on my rounds that the elder generation holds so much more affection for their postie than younger generations do, and perhaps this is part of the reason. There is not, after all, much inspiration to be found about modern, privatised Royal Mail, especially when compared with that of a Royal Mail that once delivered to the trenches.

That being said, the posties are bracing themselves. It's just six weeks to Christmas and, after the year we've had, everyone's preparing themselves for an onslaught.

Are you still there?

P.

LETTER THIRTY-SIX

20th November

I've been called many things since I became a postie, not many of which are flattering, let alone printable. It wasn't until today, however, that I was accused of *not* being a postman at all, which is a strange thing to suggest of someone who is walking around posting letters, decked to the high heavens in what looks suspiciously like a postman's uniform. Then again, I was working in the more, shall we say, *interesting* part of Brislington.

The office is in disarray as Christmas looms: more parcels arrive every hour, higher numbers of posties are sick every morning, and the managers scratch their heads harder with each passing minute, as the warehouse becomes more congested than the A37 on a Friday afternoon. The management adopt a different strategy every day, which really means there's no strategy at all and that we're just fighting fire. One of the managers, in typical fashion, noticed this morning that the frames for Walks Forty-One and Forty-Two were sagging dangerously under the weight of so many letters and that there wasn't room for a single extra envelope in the slots. Not one. With this alarming sight before them they quite literally grabbed the nearest postie – which just so happened to be me, arriving cheerfully and unsuspecting – and hurled me in the direction of this monstrosity.

"Don't worry about the parcels," they said breathlessly and a tad dramatically. "Just take what letters you can, quickly!" Then they turned on their heel to go and have a lie down from the shock of it all.

Seeing as I could simply tie up all the letters into bundles and get posting immediately, I figured I had an extra three hours on the streets and that, therefore, I could try and clear both frames. That is to say, I thought I could do about four days of work in one shift and this was an error. It is not the first time I have made this error and it won't be the last, but it is a tricky one to avoid. When it's only 6.30am and you are fresh and energetic, it's easy to fool yourself into thinking you can move mountains. This morning I genuinely tried to move a mountain of post and it nearly broke me. Or rather, a young angry lad nearly broke me.

It was an unmitigated disaster. Loops that should have taken me half an hour instead took a full turn of the clock's hour hand because the letters were so copious. Bundles of letters for one road had to be split down into four quarters, for the satchel could not hold so much post. And the normal brief and pleasant exchanges with the public became long-winded complaints about how they hadn't seen a postie in so long that they thought Royal Mail might have simply given up. It's hard to shoulder these grumbles when you are trying so hard to fix what you did not break, but the grumbles have to be directed at someone, I suppose. Much like the manager grabbed the nearest postie to them this morning, members of the public are liable to shoot the messenger too.

By 5pm I had been on my feet for eleven hours and had

walked about fifteen miles with a heavy satchel across my shoulder. I was more than a little tired, and so I was relieved to be on my very last loop: a small street at the bottom of Sandy Park Road.

Posties never intend to make mistakes, but they happen – and on days like today they are inevitable. As I made my way along the road I headed up number eighteen's garden path, when I should have walked by and gone to number nineteen. But every other house had had letters today, so I was in the habit of just going to every door. Anyway, I own that I made the mistake of going to number eighteen's door and consequently putting a large amount of post for number nineteen in the wrong letterbox.

Just as I reached the end of the cul-de-sac, the door of number eighteen flew open. The occupant started yelling at me from his doorway and I quickly realised what had happened. What I didn't realise very quickly, however, was that I was shouting back at him, and by the time I did realise it, it was too late. I should have ignored him, of course, but I'd spent the day being reprimanded by the very public that I was breaking my back to try and serve, and here was some dingbat shouting at me.

I honestly don't know what it was I had shouted, other than it was something sarcastic: any wit that I woke up with this morning had certainly deserted me and sarcasm was all that remained. I didn't swear and I wasn't aggressive, but I did shout because he was some distance away and I foolishly felt I needed to be heard. Well, shouting is aggressive by its very nature and it invited trouble.

From the corner of my eye I saw him coming down the road in quick, angry strides as I crossed to the other side of the cul-de-sac. *Oh, this is not ideal*, I thought, or something equally understated.

I posted great wedges of post to a couple more houses

and as I was turning away from the third letterbox he was there. Right there. Just-one-foot-away-kind-of-there. He was visibly seething: his body agitated and fidgeting, his face pouting oddly and his mouth swearing profusely. Dog threats aside, it was the first time my guard has come up and I started – as one cannot help but do in these situations – calculating outcomes. He was, I observed with some relief, about the same height but slighter than me and, judging by his glazed eyes most likely drunk or high. He was younger than me – probably early twenties – and he oozed a youthful anger with nothing to direct it towards other than mislaid letters and a tired postman.

I stepped around him and continued posting down the street, but he followed and continued swearing and yelling at me about the letters. Finding no bite, he changed tack:

"Who ar' ya then? Wos yer name?" He started prodding a finger into my back. "You ain't even a postman. Where's yer ID?" He shoved a hand into my satchel, presumably hoping my ID would magically appear.

How did it get to this, I thought to myself, as he prodded away at me. I was well aware that any escalation, no matter how little part I played in it, would be far more consequential to me. While he seemed to have nothing to lose, I could almost hear the Bristol tabloids licking their lips at the idea of a postman in a brawl in the street. I kept posting, kept ignoring him and inadvertently infuriated him even more.

At the end of the next garden path he stood squarely in front of me, arms crossed, mouth still pouting madly and demanded: "Name and ID."

"I don't have ID," I sighed at him. "I'm just a postie."

(As it goes, technically I should have ID, but management has never given it to me. Alas, I didn't think this detail was something that would help in the given moment.)

"Wos yer name?" He repeated. "I'm gonna report you to the Post Office."

I also didn't think it would be of much help to explain to him that I had nothing to do with the Post Office. Royal Mail split from the Post Office in 2012. Although I didn't mind the idea of this physical altercation becoming a bureaucratic one.

"Go for it," I said, and gave him my name.

"Oh, a likely story!" he exclaimed accusingly. "Tom the postie! What do you take me for mate? Give me your ID!"

And there it was, the strangest accusation ever levelled at me, and with it a sudden and severe tiredness washed over me and I wanted only to go home.

"I'm just trying to do my job," I replied. I won't tell you what he thought about my efforts at doing my job, but suffice to say he didn't hold them in very high regard.

"That's fine," I muttered, and he let me ease past him and carry on down the street.

He retreated across the road and I heard his door slam shut. A few moments later, when I was a little further along the houses, the top window of his house opened and his shouts came echoing down the road. I can't be sure what he said, but I like to think he thanked me on behalf of Brislington (the more interesting part) for working a twelve-hour day to try and get them their post, even if it did mean that the odd mistake was made, given I was – after all – only human. Yes, I'm pretty sure that's what he said.

You know the drill,

P.

LETTER THIRTY-SEVEN

3rd December

In forlorn and deep voices this morning, the posties sang along to the radio:

"It's beginning to look a lot like Christmas,
Everywhere you go..."

If Christmas looks like anything in particular, to a postie it looks like a warehouse stacked to the rafters with parcels, of frames bulging with post, and of colleagues shuffling around the office scowling and muttering obscenities.

It is a relief to get out to the streets and take in a great big gulp of cold air until it burns at some of the lesser-visited pockets of my lungs. Autumn has, you must have noticed, been a spectacular explosion of fiery colours and it glows brightly in my eyes as I walk along leaf-strewn streets. The green city of Bristol has been turned red and orange as autumn decays the leaves once more, falling to the ground where they yellow, then they brown and then seem to disappear altogether.

I am invariably a chipper kind of chap in the first hours on the street, body and brain still mostly keeping up with one another. But as I tire the cold seems to make its way through my layers one by one, until it has bitten into not only my skin but into my bones. *Biting cold* seems such an appropriate turn of phrase, I thought to myself this afternoon, as I stared mindlessly at the front door I had just knocked on. When the atmosphere is icy like this it arrests you, clenches you, really gets its teeth into you, you know? By this point of the day I relish the rush of warmth that tumbles out of people's front doors, and resent the return to the cold pavement where my breath fills the air and the atmosphere nips at me once more.

The next front door I rat-a-tat-tatted on this afternoon took a long time to answer. As I stood patiently, my eyes rested on a comfortable spot in the indiscernible mid-distance, my warm breath formed temporary clouds before me and my mind slowed until it was as active as my planted feet.

The front door slammed open abruptly. A balaclava-clad man ran out into the road. He held a brown and bulging bag and took off down the street. Before my mind was aware this was the decision I had opted for, my legs were carrying my body after him. The man turned left at the end of the road and my feet slapped noisily in pursuit. I rounded the corner and saw him running up the hill ahead. The Shepherd and his dog were on the corner. I sprinted after the robber, my own satchel weighing me down as much as the contents of his own bounty.

"Where ya going, Bill?" Called the Shepherd.

"Argh!" I responded, the cold air burning my throat.

"Woof," encouraged the dog.

The robber hung a right and saw me chasing him. The white of his eyes grew bigger beneath the black material and that spurred me on. I turned right after him and was closing in. Somewhere in the distance I heard the familiar throes of a wolf whistle thrust from the improbable beak of a parrot. I ran harder still. I was almost close enough to take a running leap at his legs. To send him sprawling across the tarmac as I landed neatly on top of him. To sit on him until someone nearby called the fuzz. Nearly there now. One, two, three—

"Hello?" said the woman at the door I was, it transpires, still standing at. "Hello there, Mr Postman?"

I blinked. Temporary clouds were still forming before my face. The balaclava-clad man was nowhere to be seen.

"Sorry," I spluttered. But really I was only sorry it had all been a dream.

"Don't worry, dear," said the woman kindly.

"Awfully sorry," I repeated. "Must have drifted off there."

She smiled sweetly.

"Ah!" I cried after a moment longer. "Your parcel!" I thrust the parcel in her direction.

She nodded at me, took her parcel and closed the door. I pictured herself shaking her head as she withdrew into her warm abode, away from both me and the frozen air of mid-autumn. "Postmen falling asleep on their own two feet?"

Whatever next,

P.

P.S. Can you believe it? They've got a vaccine for us! I think we might be alright.

LETTER THIRTY-EIGHT

9th December

"Always moanin', you are," Big Barry said to Little Larry, as they rattled their Yorks out into the December drizzle.

"There's always more moanin' to be 'ad," Little Larry pointed out, and that rather settled that. As I squeezed the last few parcels into the back of my van, which bulged ominously this morning, I thought to myself that right there could be the postie's motto: "There's always more moanin' to be 'ad".

I took the obligatory running jump at my van doors to get them shut, rattled the York into the corner of the yard where they were haphazardly strewn and headed to the urinals to find out the weather forecast for the day. I returned to the van vesically relieved, meteorologically informed and audibly jangling.

Jangling? Yes jangling, for today I had so many sets of keys about my person I sounded like Father Christmas himself (who, incidentally, really doesn't pull his considerable weight at this time of year at all).

On some rounds, we have to collect the letters from the postboxes. In the morning when you go to the cubby hole in the corner where Bert lives (he actually could live there for all I know, for I have seldom seen him outside of it), he'll also give you the keys to these postboxes. The keys are great big long things that look like they open heavy and important doors, and perhaps in some ways that is exactly what they do.

When you heave open the heart of the postboxes they groan pleasingly for they have been there a long time and they see as much of the maintenance man as Bert sees of the great outdoors. There in the bottom of this tall red tube is a handful of letters and you pluck them out to put them in a pocket of your satchel. Having heaved the great door shut again and locked it, you continue your day, and at the end of it you get a little reminder on your electronic device that you must put those letters in a certain place in the sorting office so that they can continue their onward journey. In fairness to Royal Mail, it's a good system and it works – and it's not that often you can say that.

Until Christmas time, that is. At Christmas time you cannot simply swing the postbox open, because inside of it a colossal number of letters are eagerly awaiting the opportunity to pour out of the postbox at a rate of knots – and if you are not wise to it then you are in trouble.

It happened to me last year. Little did I know quite how committed to Christmas card writing this island was, until I opened a postbox one December day and found myself being carried down the street on an avalanche of white envelopes like snow from a mountaintop. Or so it seemed to me, at least. It was a windy day too – of course it was a windy day – and so having plugged the flow of letters and hastily closed the door again, I had to scamper around snatching soggy Christmas cards up from the pavements, some of which had escaped a great distance from the postbox. I lost about fifteen minutes picking them all up, and once I had collected them I didn't have enough room in my satchel to take those that remained in the postbox. So, I had to finish the loop, get to the van and then drive back to the postbox, as I really should have done from the very beginning, such that I could carefully collect the rest from the heart of this mighty tube sticking out of the street.

After the panic of it had all faded, an anger came to me. Not an anger with the people sending them: they are only being nice and following these expectations we have created. It was an anger towards whoever, or whatever, created this expectation in the first place. I was compelled to dig back through the annals of time to find out who was to blame for this invention.

It turns out it was a nincompoop of a man called Henry Cole. In 1843, he thought up the idea of encouraging a greetings card over Christmas. Uniform penny postage had been introduced three years before, meaning a letter could now be sent to and from anywhere in the country for the price of just a penny. The postal system, therefore, was no longer the reserve of the gentry, but suddenly accessible to millions of people and the volume of letters exploded. I can imagine the posties now, sat around in the canteen on one of their allotted breaks, moaning at the sudden rise in letters ("there's always more moanin' to be 'ad", one of them would have said). The general public really bought into the penny postage, for the volume of letters doubled within a year of its introduction and you can bet your last penny that Royal Mail didn't double the number of staff to deal with it.

Well, Henry Cole saw this as an opening and shortly thereafter commissioned the first Christmas cards. Their popularity was significant, instant and evidently long lasting, because here I am now, some 180 years on, delivering the sodding things. The tradition of sending Christmas cards remains as rooted in our culture as the postboxes in the pavement: both go a long way down. Indeed, you wouldn't want to reverse into a postbox, for it is as deep in the ground as it is high in the air, making it as sturdy as – if not more so – any nearby tree.

Incidentally, an avalanche of letters is not all that I have found in a postbox in the past. I have also come across chocolate wrappers, although to date no chocolate. I have discovered a mobile phone, which I was so surprised to see that I simply left it where it was, in case its owner with an impossibly long, thin and flexible arm wanted to reach down into the depths of the postbox to retrieve it. I have since concluded that this old Nokia phone was most likely ditched by somebody who sold things of an illegal nature and who had become spooked by a passing police car, but I have no definite proof. I wasn't back on that walk again for a long time and forgot to ask around as to what became of the phone: it wasn't there the next time I was on that duty.

Best of all, however, I have found letters written by children to Father Christmas in postboxes. At least, I assume they are written by children. They are often letters without envelopes, just A4 pieces of paper covered in looping crayon squiggles depicting all of the writer's hopes and dreams for the morning of the twenty-fifth day of the twelfth month. The letters are invariably folded clumsily and crumpled enthusiastically into the postbox, and you can almost smell the hope on them that – despite everything – the author of that letter has been good enough this year after all.

Softheartedly,

P.

P.S. The first Covid vaccine was given to a ninety-year old lady yesterday, by the name of Margaret Keenan. I don't normally believe in Christmas miracles but...

A SHORT MISSIVE ON THE
FATE OF A POSTBOX

Dear Sir,

Indeed, I am acutely aware of how ironic it would have been had I reversed into that postbox today. Nonetheless, I thank you for pointing it out and for drawing most of south Bristol's attention to it. One can never gesticulate too much or shout too loudly when a postbox is in danger, or if – as in this case – my ongoing employment is one crumpled postvan away from jeopardy.

Your repentant and blushing postie,

P.

LETTER THIRTY-NINE

16th December

I fell asleep last night to the distant sound of sorting machines churning through tomorrow's post and the wheels of the Royal Mail trucks rumbling across the dark plains, their suspension creaking under the weight of tradition and habit. My dreams were fraught with dogs appearing around improbable corners, dump trucks unloading great waves of letters on top of me and impossible parcel-built mazes stretching up to the warehouse ceiling.

This morning's alarm was something of a relief, even if it did precede a finger-numbing, face-freezing cycle into work in the cold, quiet hours of the day. When I reached the relative sanctuary of the sorting office, I wasn't there long. One of the managers – looking even more sleep deprived and haggard than me – pointed meekly to some parcel-laden Yorks in the corner and pleaded with me to just take them and do what I could. I was happy to get out of the sorting office – the atmosphere was as tense as ever and there was no room to move for the amount of stuff that had arrived that morning. I piled the parcels in the van as best I could, ran my shoulder to the back door, and was driving up into the dark and hitherto undisturbed streets of Knowle in no time.

I had to wait a few minutes for it to turn to 7am: the policy is to not knock on doors any earlier than that. But even then, in the depths of winter, it is still solidly black and people are not awake yet. Nobody wants to be woken up by a loud rapping at the door at that time of day, at this time of year. For the first hour I am met with dressing-gowned figures in unlit doorways, the red of their bleary eyes peering out worriedly into the now dark-blue dawn. A mixture of relief and anger rings through their voice as they realise who I am.

"You scared the 'ell out of oi!"

"What toime do you call this?"

"This is too early!"

All common reprimands. It doesn't occur to them that they're the ones who have ordered the parcel, or that for me to be there at their door at that time means I must have been awake far longer, or that they might not be the only ones in this dense, immense city who have opted for online delivery, rather than going to the shops themselves at a more sociable hour.

I force myself to make no comment, because I am sure that there is no reserve of politeness left in me. I hand them the parcel and disappear into the dark street. As I'm mentally preparing myself for the next scolding, I have to remind myself that the general public have no way of knowing what a nightmare it is for delivery drivers at this time of year, and I force myself to try and be more understanding of their situation. I also can't help but wish they would extend me the same empathy.

As day emerges – grey and damp – people become a little

friendlier, but I know this is the sweet spot of the morning: a golden hour where people have woken at their chosen time, are having their breakfast and are readying themselves for the day. This is when I can get rid of a lot of parcels, before the rush hour starts and people have left for work. I work furiously and relentlessly in this period, because soon I will be knocking on a lot of doors where nobody is home, and then I have to go knock on a neighbour's door, and then I have to go *back* to the initial door to let them know the neighbour has it or that maybe the neighbour wasn't in either. This is an infuriatingly slow part of the day and it will be the case until about 5pm, when people have started to come home and are glad to be there and glad to see me, and another golden hour begins.

"Oh," they'll say, "still working? Late for you, isn't it?" But I won't be able to bring myself to anything more than a grunt, because I am exhausted and the van still has plenty of parcels in it. Since darkness has fallen again I cannot see the addresses on the boxes in the van any more and it takes much longer to find the right one. When I miss parcels and realise twenty minutes later that I have to double back, I almost scream in frustration because I am cold and exhausted and there is nothing I can do but keep on delivering. And now I cannot see the numbers on the houses either, so I often park fifty metres away from a house accidentally, and find myself running between the van and front doors. And because it is rush hour again and people are coming home to their small residential streets, my van is blocking the road and people are getting upset and impatient with me. They beep their horns and shake their heads in disgust, and I want to yell at them but I know that I can't. Instead, I'll moan about it in a letter.

When the last parcel is delivered, there is no satisfaction and no relief. As I drive back to the sorting office I know that this hellish day has not made the slightest difference to the volume of parcels that will still be there, because as hard as we are all working, there are simply too many. While those at the top of Royal Mail roll in the profit of all these parcels, and the shareholders are kept happy, the posties who are breaking their backs out on the streets are going home stressed and unappreciated, and no better off than when they put their shoulder to the wheel however many years ago.

Grumpily,

P.

P.S. In brighter news, they're relaxing the rules so we can be with our families. Will it ever have meant so much to people as it will this year, for families to sit around the table and share Christmas together? The mere thought of it makes me weep, but then I am very tired.

A SHORT MISSIVE ON THE WHEREABOUTS OF FATHER CHRISTMAS

Dear Father Christmas,
    Where the bloody hell are you?

Your peeved postie,

P.

LETTER FORTY

We gave up trying to deliver post about a week ago. Or rather, the managers haven't told us to take any out since then, because Royal Mail is unashamedly prioritising parcels and so we are now not posties but parcelies, and there are a lot of letters in the office not going anywhere. Even with this strategy, however, we cannot cope. This morning the manager turned three lorries – brimming with Christmas detritus – back to Bristol's main sorting office, because we simply had nowhere to put it all.

While letters can be stored away in dusty corners, parcels by their nature are imposing and demand delivery with their mere chunkiness, gobbling up the space if we refuse to take them to their destinations. Even a few thousand letters can be stacked around the office – under the frames, up in the rafters with the pigeons, next to Arthur in the urinals – but if we allow the parcels to stack upwards from the floor as quickly as the rain falls on the roof, either the floor or the roof are in trouble. Also, from the public's point of view, letters have the unfortunate – albeit wonderful – quality of mysteriousness and a proclivity towards surprise: people tend not to know they are coming. The progress of a parcel, on the other hand, can be watched on a screen as if it were a horse in the Grand National and everybody wants theirs to come in first.

Lastly, and rather cynically, it has been pointed out that letters don't make Royal Mail a whole lot of money these days, whereas parcels do. Whether or not we have been delivering letters for more than 500 years, there is no sentiment to be found when sorting offices across the country are drowning in an ocean of indulgence. Indeed, the more the posties are drowning in parcels, the more those at the top are swimming in profits and they don't mind that too much at all. Indeed, the company knows that parcels are the future so, as I say, we don't post letters any more.

But, then, who writes letters any more? Somewhere along the line we stopped writing letters to each other and started ordering parcels for ourselves online, and that feels like a tragedy of Shakespearean magnitude. The humble letter, neat and compact, can hold more weight, more joy, more life, than anything that can be bought online. Letters have started revolutions, ended wars and communicated world-changing ideas around the globe. They have ignited romance, fused life-long friendships and eased breaking hearts. They have, admittedly, done all of the opposites too: wars have started and hearts have broken at the stroke of a pen and the lick of a stamp. But this is precisely what makes them so meaningful and so much more like real life than the new Juicer 3000, say, that with the click of a mouse can be with you tomorrow. Even if it can produce tasty, nutritious juice out of your unwanted apple stalk.

Amidst all this, the parcelies are occasionally chipper and can have their moments. In a rare instance of a not-

Christmas song coming on the radio this morning, they found their voices:

"Islands in the stream,
Tha' iz what we are!"

They couldn't see each other, such were the walls of parcels around each of them...

"No one in between,
'ow can we be wrong!"

But that just made them sing louder so that they might be heard...

"Sail away with oi,
To another world!"

But posties are not heard, they are only ever seen...

"And we rely on each other, uh-hah!
From one postie to another, uh-hah!"

And that seems true of workers across the country: seen but not heard. A rush of red as the postie hurries past the window, a blur of burgundy as a shop assistant dashes along an aisle, a flurry of fluorescence as the bin collector disappears down the road. Workers providing key services to the proper and healthy functioning of society, and yet the value of their contribution is systematically under-appreciated by the very system they serve. Perhaps society doesn't hold much respect for these jobs because they seem menial and therefore easy, and anyway they are ripe for automation so those who are doing them now are really only filling the gap until the robots do it all for us.

Well, maybe the robots will do it all for us one day, but I for one suspect that day remains a long way off, and in any case these are still hardworking people and they're being left behind as the world accelerates into the unknown. These workers are like the roots of city trees supporting ancient structures, while each year a new layer of tarmac is smothered over the top of them. But the roots keep on pushing back, reaching up to the surface, and the pavements are cracking.

Mind the gap,

P.

P.S. A package of parcelies, perhaps?

❧ V ❧
WINTER, ONCE MORE

As long as there are postmen, life will have zest.

William James

LETTER FORTY-ONE

21st December

It is no coincidence that we celebrate Christmas at the darkest moment of the year.

The sun has already set on this shortest day and the winter solstice will have been missed by most in this screen-obsessed age, but the ancient peoples were acutely aware of such things. They couldn't help but be. To them, winter solstice might have been the day that the sun spent the least amount of time in the sky, but it was also the day that they started to invite more sunlight back into their lives as they looked forward. That in itself, the ancients decided, was cause for celebration and celebrate they did. In Ancient Rome, for example, the festival of Saturnalia was a bonanza of gift-giving, feast-gobbling and game-playing, which all sounds suspiciously and wonderfully Christmassy to me.

But of course it takes a lot of work to have a celebration, and for those to whom the work falls it can be a tad testing. Hence why the posties were to be found particularly irate this morning, engaged in a furious row of the upmost importance.

"You've got it all wrong," Little Larry was bristling. "You wanna go right out and post to Bamfield Road first, then come back this side of the road that goes to the airport and do all the rest last."

"Why would I do Bamfield first?" Gary shot back. "That's ridiculous, with all they parcels and walking round the 'ouses an' tha'."

"Yeah, what you on about, Larry!" Big Barry joined the fray. "Bamfield first? Never 'eard anything like it! That's stupid, that's wha' that is."

"'xactly," said Gary.

"It ain't," said Little Larry. "Makes perfect sense to I. Gets it done."

"It's all gotta be done," Big Barry pointed out.

"No it ain't," said Gary, now turning on Big Barry. "I ain't takin' all tha'. Won't be 'ome until next year if I take all tha'."

"Well I'm taking all mine, Gary," said Big Barry. "Christmas, innit?"

"Sod Christmas," replied Gary. "I 'ate it."

Their dispute had begun as I pushed through the swinging doors this morning, but it's been weeks since the doors actually did any swinging. An unmovable mountain of parcels has formed in the warehouse and long put a stop to that. I could go neither under it, nor around it, so I ascended the mountain of said parcels, still clad in my woolly hat and thermals and as I reached the height of the rafters I imagined myself as seen from the foot of the mountain: an intrepid climber or perhaps a mountain goat. Either way, at the apex of this parcel peak I rummaged around and found a package that would serve as a sledge. Positioning myself carefully atop it, nodding coolly to the onlooking pigeons, I then rode it down the other side of the mountain, where I arrived in a heap before my parcel-ladened frame.

There are a lot of parcels in the warehouse at the moment. Many of them won't be making it to their destination by the end of the year, let alone by Christmas Day. All of this, needless to say, has rather gotten under the skin of the posties and I was vaguely glad to get away from the tension of the sorting office. Then again, out and about on the streets wasn't a whole lot better. For one thing, 'out and about' does not feel very 'out' at all at the moment. The December sky is so oppressive that I want to climb inside the boxes I am delivering, for I am sure I would feel less claustrophobic in one of them. Perhaps I'll open one at the bottom of the mountain tomorrow and crawl into it, safe in the knowledge that I won't be bothered for at least another week in there.

Anyway, I must bid you farewell for I have another letter to write. It's not all about you, you know. I made a collection from a postbox earlier and among the hundreds of other letters was a piece of paper from a child to Father Christmas. It near enough broke my heart – I am, like the rest, feeling quite tender at this time of year – and so I have decided to reply to it myself.

May your boomerang return to you,

P.

P.S. Christmas, as you will have no doubt heard, was cancelled yesterday. It's the U-turn to end all U-turns, and the country is in despair. The thought of Christmas together was the fuel that the population was running on for these past months, and yesterday it was cruelly snatched away from us at the eleventh hour.

LETTER FORTY-TWO

22nd December

The girl had asked for a unicorn puzzle, a Christmas decoration and some other bits and bobs. As I read it I thought about how, back in the day, Royal Mail had a department that responded to children's letters to Father Christmas. I thought about how that was a sweet thing, but then felt unsure as to whether I thought that it was a good use of the taxpayer's money. Then I felt sad because I had allowed a thing such as taxes to infringe on what was really a very sweet thing in an otherwise salty world. So I sat for a moment and admired the letter, all swirly writing and different coloured felt-tip pens, and then I thought, well, maybe I could reply to it? What a nice thing that would be, if one were a little girl or boy, to get a reply from Father Christmas. So I rummaged around and found some felt tips and I started penning a reply in my hopeless, childlike handwriting, which I think proved to be quite useful for once for the little girl would probably believe it more.

I wrote it as if Christmas had already passed. As you

know, I have inside knowledge on these things, and I can guarantee that no letters posted today will be arriving for at least another week, such is the state of affairs. It's terrible.

As I walked through the brisk winter air this morning to pop my version of Father Christmas's reply in the postbox, I felt Christmas wash over me. The celebration I have spent the month loathing came suddenly to me in its familiar but ineluctable heartwarming way. All it took was this one small act of kindness, but that's precisely what Christmas is, isn't it? The accumulation of many small acts of kindness. And perhaps, I thought to myself as I turned to walk home, therein lies what it is to be a good postie too? A human being capable of kindness.

To be a postie is to be confronted with the potential for hundreds of acts of kindness each day. These acts can range from chasing burglars (actual ones) down the street, to pretending to reply to a child's letter to Father Christmas, to stopping to let a pedestrian cross Wells Road. It could even be as simple as taking half a second more to not crumple someone's letter through the letterbox: it might be the beat of the butterfly's wing that stops that person coming home and losing their rag with the world. Rarely can a postie's act – rarely can a *person's* act – be the show-stopping, kitten-saving, crowd-winning moment of heroism that might make it into the news. But the accumulation of a hundred small acts? Well, that's the difference between returning to the sorting office with a fully loaded van and returning with an empty one. It could also be the difference between how heavily the world weighs on one's own chest: to be kind to others is also to be kind to oneself. When one realises this, one can have Christmas all year round.

What it is to be a good postie, then, is no different than what it is to be a good human. Unfortunately, to be a good human is not always the most straightforward of things either.

In my humble but impeccable opinion,

P.

LETTER FORTY-THREE

23rd December

Last year I made it to Christmas Eve day before a mince pie reduced me to a blubbering mess. This year I made it to the eve of Christmas Eve before a fall, a puddle and a gastropod-inspired-epiphany got the better of me.

I was asked to deliver parcels across two walks. About 15 sacks sat in the corner bursting at the seams with small packages, having been roundly ignored for a fortnight, and some nitwit of a manager had decided it was I who should tackle it. In such moments I often wonder who it is I have upset to be bestowed these impossible tasks, but then I look around and realise everybody else has been burdened with equally unachievable undertakings. Phew, I think to myself, we're all equally doomed.

Off I went into the dreary December weather. It was grey and had the look of a day that might be mild, but was in fact terrifically cold in a way we haven't seen of late. My van creaked under the weight of the load and my bones at the temperature of the air, and I was acutely aware that I was about to have a really unpleasant time.

At the start of each loop I strung two satchels of parcels about my bowing neck. A postie does not normally walk from house to house with two satchels of parcels but, as the parcels were as numerous as the letters normally are, I was left with little choice. I smartly thrust each package into the surprised hands of those who answered their doors, before staggering back to the street, the weight of Christmas swinging on my back. I'd turn onto the pavement and hear the drop of parcels out of my pouch as if I were Hansel or Gretel sprinkling breadcrumbs behind me, leaving a trail so that I might find my way back to the van. Alas, I had to stoop to pick them up and in doing so more parcels cascaded from the pouch.

I continued in this vein for hours, down freezing cold roads under a snow-white sky. I rapped at doors, toddled back down gardens and dropped parcels every few metres. At about midday, reaching desperately down for the thousandth time to pick up more escaped packages, I lost my balance and fell squarely into a puddle.

I wasn't in any rush to get out of this puddle. Instead, I sat in it and asked myself, what was all this for? All this rushing around, delivering all this *stuff* that people were so desperate to have? When would it all end? At Christmas? Well, clearly not. People are insatiable. This would never stop, I thought to myself in puddle-strewn despair, and there was so much sadness that I didn't know what to do next.

It was at this fateful moment that the answer crawled out in front of me. I chuckled as I watched it emerge before my eyes, where it had been this whole time if only I had taken a moment to pay it attention. I let out that chuckle and I sat chuckling in this puddle until I laughed. I laughed until I was creasing over sideways and it was no longer clear whether the water on my face was from tears of madness, falling rain or splashes of puddle.

All these days looking out for them, all these careful steps taken to avoid their paths, all the times I'd bent over to pick one up and put them out of harm's way and I'd never thought how alike we were. They with their shell on their backs and we with our pouches on ours, both patrolling the streets in vast numbers, both barely noticed.

Our one-footed friends. Those iconic creatures that cover the country as completely as posties, but are seldom seen together unless one happens to inspect a tomato plant, or watch them race up the walls and gather on the pavements as the rain falls. They go about their days at their own pace, diligently pushing themselves into every nook and cranny, leaving no residency untouched. Ubiquitous and harmless, this is an animal that posties have been paired with since the advent of the email, when the letters that we delivered became known as *snailmail*.

As the snail moved out across the pavement before me, skirting the distant shores of my puddle, I saw that there was a thing or two we could learn from this humble mollusc. We move so fast all the time, always feeling the pressure to jump from one thing to the next in every aspect of our lives: from home to work and work to home; from door to door and street and street; from this thought to that one, and that want to the next need. We chase and chase as if we might finally get all the things done, as if we might finally fulfil all our impulses and desires, and at last enter into a part of our lives where we can simply enjoy it.

The humble snail is wiser than us in this. The snail has learnt that to go faster is only to accelerate everything around you, and to take you further away from the truth, which is that we are already in the part of our lives that we can simply enjoy. We just have to slow down, even if that means retreating into our shells from time to time.

Do you know what a group of snails is called? A walk of snails. How brilliant, I thought to myself, still gazing at the slow-moving exoskeleton. Brilliant for two reasons. One, to walk is to move slowly, and how wonderfully appropriate that is to the snail. And two, a snail quite clearly is *not* walking at all, and so how wonderfully *inappropriate* a walk of snails is too! Leopards may leap and squirrels may scurry, but snails do not walk and therein lies everything I want from my collective nouns.

So, I have a proposition for the nerds behind the pages of the Oxford English Dictionary. For too long have posties collected every morning in warehouses across the country and had no name by which to call themselves. For too long have they stood on a picket line as a group and there not been a word with which to refer to them as one. But, from the depths of a great puddle today I believe I surfaced with the very word that they've been denied for more than 500 years. I believe we should henceforth be known collectively as a walk of posties.

Postman puddle,

P.

A SHORT MISSIVE ON
REASONS TO BE A SNAIL

Dear Arthur,

I was sitting in my van inhaling a thirty-second sandwich the other day and watching you work. You were so *slow*. This is why the manager has made me take your parcels: because you won't have the time to do it. I was annoyed with you at first, but as I watched I came to see why you were slow. You're of the old breed. I don't mean *old*. I mean you still take the time to chat with the people, to give their dog a treat and to close their gate.

In the sorting office, where the world marches madly on, you are considered less useful by the day. But what if it is not that you are too slow, but that the rest of us are running too fast? I see now that we are colluding in the acceleration of the world when we fail to appreciate what you do. I send my heartfelt apologies to you.

But there's nothing I can do to stop it.

Helplessly,

P.

LETTER FORTY-FOUR

24th December

It's not the twenty-fourth of December unless you hear the hallowed words...

"It was Christmas Eve babe, in the drunk tank,
An old man said to oi, won't see another one..."

It's been a year to the day since my first letter to you. So much has changed, so much is the same: such is the life of the postie. Christmas Eve again but, a little like the old man in The Pogues' 'Fairytale of New York', I'm not sure I'll see another one. Not in this job. I am exhausted by the workload and exasperated by the state of affairs. But, as ever, I was delighted to find the warehouse in full swing as those non-swinging doors didn't swing this morning.

"Got on a lucky one, came in eigh'een-to-one!
I've got a feelin', this year's for oi and you..."

We've been pushed to the limits this year. I know the whole country has, I know people have had it really bad, but I hope they remember how hard the posties have worked for them, how they have tried their best. Tomorrow the people should be with their loved ones, cherishing one another and all that the blood, sweat and tears of some singing red elves has brought to their door.

"They got cars big as bars, they got rivers of gold,
But the wind goes right through ye, ain't no place for the old..."

Patricia and Neil, my once trainees, waltzed in the corner as they arranged the last load of parcels before Christmas. Both of them donned a Christmas hat, their two white baubles swinging madly around as they pirouetted between the pillars.

"You were handsome, you were pretty, queen of Bristol city,
When the band finished playing, they 'owled out for more..."

Little Larry, Big Barry and Gary roared along as they sorted their letters. Their eyes skimmed the addresses while their brains dashed around the streets that they knew so well and their feet danced across the warehouse floor so that they could slot letters into the appropriate centimetres. Their heads were down, hard at work as always, but it was Christmas Eve and their spirits were up. We were nearly there.

"The boys of the Bristol city choir
Were singing, Galway Bay!
And the bells were ringing out
For Christmas Day..."

As the violins faded wistfully out, Bert emerged from his lair and cried, "Up the workers!" It got such a big cheer that nobody could hear his punchline: "Have you seen any?"

Have you seen any workers? I have. I've seen workers who have carried a nation on their shoulders this year. I've seen workers turn up for duty long before the sun came up and leave long after it had gone back down. I've seen workers turned white by the frost and red by the sun. I saw workers this year until a mountain of parcels arrived in our sorting office and blocked them all from view, and then it was only on my ascents of this mountain did I spot colleagues in distant corners of the warehouse, trying to bring some sort of order to their impossible workload.

As such, it is not quiet in the office like it was last Christmas Eve. Nobody finished early today like in years gone by, and when we returned to the warehouse the mountain was still there and for the first time ever we had failed. Failed in our efforts to deliver Christmas on time. But the writing was on the wall weeks ago and we'd long come to accept it. As ever, this morning we took what we could, but it was Christmas Eve and we didn't want to break our backs.

I was on Walk Thirty-Six, a random one for me to be assigned given that Little Larry or Big Barry usually take charge of it, but they had been sent to some other corner of the city today. As such, it was with no small degree of guilt – not to mention gratitude – that I accepted a box of chocolates from an elderly gentleman on their round today. He hurried out of his front door – armed with a walking stick in one hand and a neatly wrapped circular parcel in the other – and wheezed a soft shout in my direction. I went to him and he bestowed me with the gift. He was breathless but his eyes twinkled a thank you, and the warm feeling of Christmas swelled in me again.

When I returned to the sorting office I took the gift to the frame and left it with a note to Little Larry and Big Barry, telling them which house it was from so they could thank him themselves after Christmas. I hope I will be there to see them fight over it.

A few posties were coming and going, all of them ghosts of their former selves. We smiled meekly at one another and wished each other a Merry Christmas. But we'll be back in a couple of days to chip away at the mountain again.

A manager was chatting with another postie nearby, waiting for the last of us to leave so he could lock up the building and go home. I asked him what he was doing for Christmas and he just replied, "Sleep", with neither a morsel of irony or even the energy to make it a verb. Simply, sleep. We all need to sleep.

As I pushed out of the doors into the darkening Christmas Eve, I sucked in a great lungful of the salty Bristol air and suddenly felt as free as if on an ocean. Time to go home, I thought to myself, and I smiled.

Merry Christmas to you,

P.

POSTSCRIPT

How often does what a writer most want to convey live in the postscript? Whatever was contained in Cecelia Ahern's letters, it's safe to assume the only words that truly mattered were the eponymous ones popularised by the film that followed her book *P.S. I Love You*. Presumably, whatever words preceded this postscript were the chitter and the chatter that wrapped themselves around this core message of adoration.

The coronavirus pandemic was relegated to the P.S.s in this bundle of letters for a similar reason. In many ways it was all that mattered in those years: an all-consuming fact around which the rest of our lives wrapped themselves. At the time of writing, nobody really wants to read a book about the pandemic. But if you are reading this, you actually just have. As with Cecelia Ahern's letters, you just didn't know the truth until you got to the end.

I couldn't have written this collection of missives had I not been a postman. That might sound obvious: to write a memoir of sorts about being a postman, one damn sure better have been a postman. Otherwise, the whole thing is a bit of a farce. But this is no such thing, for I did indeed serve my time as a postie at Bristol's southeast delivery office for the best part of three years. Three years largely dominated by the Covid-19 pandemic.

This collection of letters started whirling around my head as I was out on my rounds, but it was in the year after leaving the job that they finally found pages to be written on. The letters could never have found a page if being a postman hadn't taught me the beauty and discipline of the very early morning: this is what I mean when I say I couldn't have written it otherwise. The early morning is the only time of day I find myself capable of locating coherent thoughts in my head, sending them down my arms and tapping them out from my fingertips onto the keyboard. Magically, this all then appears on my computer screen and with some further magic down the line it becomes a book.

My alarm clock, therefore, hardly changed when I stopped being a postie. I would swing my legs out of bed before 6am, put the coffee on, and then sit for a cold, dark hour at my desk each morning. Snatching these one-hour sessions to write these letters became a haven: an hour of peace where I could try and put the complications of the world into something fun and affecting.

It is comforting to think as I write this – in another early dark, hour – that all across the country posties are arriving to work, letters are being shuffled into pigeon holes and well-known lyrics are being amusingly bastardised in every accent the UK has to offer. I may have only worked in one sorting office, but there is something that tells me all posties approach their work and their workplace in very much the same fashion: with a good deal of laughter, a fair amount of moaning and a lot of very hard work.

Since taking the dubious step from letter bringer to office worker, I have watched with dismay as Royal Mail has entered into turmoil along with so many other crucial industries across the country. There was never a strike in my years as a postie. It was a moment of national crisis and not at all the right time for industrial action when so many other important things were quickly unravelling – and when the posties and the postal network was to be instrumental to the nation's response to Covid-19.

Alongside the fear of this invisible killer among us, there was also a remarkable hope among posties that we could do something to help the country in its moment of need. Standing shoulder to shoulder on the front line, we were key workers alongside doctors and nurses, shop assistants and bin collectors, and many others. Like all of them, posties were ready to serve the public however they could.

It was disheartening to discover that the purpose we mostly served was bringing people all their online shopping, which went through the roof – quite literally, in the case of Royal Mail warehouses – during those lockdowns. We thought we might be delivering food, medicine and other essentials to keeping people going. Instead, we ended up delivering people *stuff*. Stuff that they needed to fill their unfulfilling days, thereby making our days particularly unfulfilling and indefinitely stressful. It was like a year-long Christmas.

The public were, for the most part, grateful to their posties at the time and we were glad for that. I was certain that the service we carried out in those terrible months would be remembered and that all of our previous concerns about working conditions would have been knocking on the door of public attention. After all, for a time, posties were the only other people that anyone really saw. We brought the public signs of life on the outside world, we brought them all the new hobbies they decided to pick up, and in the first half of 2021 we delivered forty-seven million letters inviting the adult population to get vaccinated and put an end to the nightmare we were all living through. Surely, I thought to myself, the posties would be rewarded?

I was incredibly wrong. As soon as the world opened up, the notion that posties were key to how people had made it through those months – how they had always made it through the months – was swiftly forgotten. Everybody wanted to ignore the fact that the pandemic had ever happened, and in doing so they forgot all those who had got them through it as well. Not just delivery workers, but all of those working in health, education and transport too. It is no coincidence that industrial action overwhelmed all of these sectors in the aftermath of Covid-19.

It is undeniably true that pressure had been building in the mail system for years before the pandemic. There were two devastatingly popular votes to strike in the preceding months. So the postal strikes that came hot on the heels of the pandemic were clearly about far more than concerns of the ensuing cost-of-living crisis. They were also about protecting thousands of jobs at risk, they were about reasonable working hours and they were about the sanctity of Sundays ("no post on Sundays", as Mr Dursley said). I don't speak for the doctors, nurses, teachers or rail staff, but their strikes were about so much more than pay too. Not that much of the media, or any of the government, have been willing to recognise that.

I wrote this bundle of letters for two reasons. One, because my experience of posting in Bristol was, for a time, a truly wonderful occupation that I wanted to share. And two, because in the time since I have left I have watched with dismay as posties have gone from being key workers to being criticised for their strike action, and I want to show my support for them.

Indeed, this bundle of letters is many things. It is an ode

to both letter writing and our uniquely human system of delivering letters worldwide. It is an ode to the outdoors and to the changing of the seasons. But more than anything else, it is an ode to key workers, who carried a nation across the void only to be left behind when the world came out the other side.

The end,

P.

WRONGS OF PASSAGE

THE TALES BEFORE BLUE EYE SAILED
AROUND THE WORLD

TOM DYMOND

WRONGS OF PASSAGE

Before he was a postman, Tom and his friend James sailed a boat barely bigger than a bathtub around the world. If you enjoyed *Letters from a Postman*, then you will love Tom's books about this wild adventure.

Wrongs of Passage: The Tales Before Blue Eye Sailed Around The World is **the free and much-loved prequel** to that adventure.

The eBook can be downloaded from Bookfunnel for free by heading to tsdymond.com/books, or by scanning the QR code below.

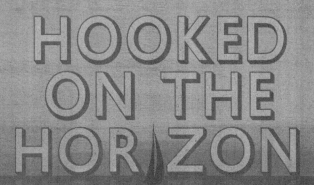

HOOKED ON THE HORIZON

SAILING BLUE EYE AROUND THE WORLD

TOM DYMOND

HOOKED ON THE HORIZON

Tom then takes the reader around the world with his hair-raising, hilarious and insightful memoir, *Hooked on the Horizon: Sailing* Blue Eye *Around the World.*

★★★★★ "It's an extraordinary book and an instant classic."

★★★★★ "One of the finest pieces of writing today... a true masterpiece."

★★★★★ "It has the hallmarks of a great travel memoir, authentically told, and able to change the reader as it did the young adventurers."

Head to tsdymond.com/books to get your copy.

REVIEWS

DID YOU ENJOY LETTERS FROM A POSTMAN?

Thank you so much for reading this book, I really hope you enjoyed it. If you did, there is something you can do for me.

Honest reviews of my book are immensely powerful things for helping other readers to find me. If you have two minutes, I would be hugely grateful if you left one on my book's Amazon page. To do so, you can scan the QR code below, and leave a review as short or as long as you please.

Thank you very, very much.

ACKNOWLEDGEMENTS

Life often gets in the way of projects like this, and each of the people central to the production of this book have certainly been through their fair share of 'life' recently. I would not have held it against any of them had they bowed out, but I am immensely grateful that none of them did. They were my key workers, and I won't forget them.

To my editor Emily Kearns, who - were she to be a postie herself - I am sure would never post a letter to the wrong house, such is the meticulousness and care with which she approaches her work. Thank you for your hard work and for reeling me in during my overly ambitious moments.

To my designer Andy Bridge, who has created a truly stunning book cover. I am hugely grateful to you for your work after the year you have had, and incredibly impressed that you were still able to produce anything at all, let alone something so beautiful. I hugely appreciate it, and you.

To my illustrator Tallulah Pomeroy, who brought the seasons to life through her wonderful drawings of a postie and an oak tree. I had a suspicion your skillset would be suitable for this, but I did not realise it would be perfect. Thank you so much.

To photographer Stuart Thomas for the pictures he took of me in Bristol in my postie uniform back in the day. A big thank you for your persistence on an ill-lit and devilishly cold winter's morning.

And last, but by no means least, thanks to my advance readers - the so-called Dymond Geezers - who selflessly proofread the final draft of these letters and offered their thoughts. Helen Andrews, Harry Clarke, Will Miller, Laura Fisher, Linda Nixon, Beryl Light, Diana Wardley, Carlton Boyce, Lester Foldi and Richard Todd: I am in your debt.

I must finally single out my grandmother and chief Dymond Geezer, Clare Waddington, for being disarmingly successful in picking up the last few errors in the text, and for doing so in record time. This book is for you, and for all of my grandparents: I am eternally grateful for all of your love and support.

ABOUT THE AUTHOR

Photographs courtesy of Stuart Thomas

Tom Dymond's days have been pleasingly scattered across the southwest of England: a childhood in Dorset, a schooling in Somerset, some further education in Devon, before eventually a settling of sorts in Bristol. More can be gleaned from his website, tsdymond.com.

Tom loves to hear from his readers. Letters are preferable, of course, but he never seems to be in one place long enough to provide a reliable address. Emails, on the other hand, tend to follow him around: tsd@tsdymond.com.

You can also connect with him on Facebook at facebook.com/tsdymondauthor, or on Instagram at @tsdymond.

Printed in Great Britain
by Amazon